why
white kids
love
HIP-HOP

Also by Bakari Kitwana

The Hip Hop Generation
The Rap on Gangsta Rap

why
white kids
love
HIP-HOP

wankstas, wiggers, wannabes,
and the new reality of race in America

bakari kitwana

BASIC
CIVITAS
BOOKS

A Member of the Perseus Books Group
New York

Books published by Basic Civitas are available at special discounts for
bulk purchases in the United States by corporations, institutions, and
other organizations. For more information, please contact the Special
Markets Department at the Perseus Books Group, 11 Cambridge Center,
Cambridge MA 02142, or call (617) 252-5298 or (800) 255-1514,
or e-mail special.markets@perseusbooks.com.

Text design by Trish Wilkinson
Set in 11.75-pt. Minion by the Perseus Books Group

Library of Congress Cataloging-in-Publication Data

Kitwana, Bakari.
    Why white kids love hip hop : wankstas, wiggers, wannabes, and the
new reality of race in America / Bakari Kitwana.
        p. cm.
    Includes index.
    ISBN 0-465-03746-1 (hardcover : alk. paper)
    1. Rap (Music)—History and criticism. 2. Rap (Music)—Political
aspects—United States. 3. Music and race. I. Title.
ML3531.K58 2005
306.4'84249—dc22

                                                                2005003553

ISBN-13 978-0-465-03746-9

05   06   07   08   /   10   9   8   7   6   5   4   3   2   1

To my mother, Dorothy Dance, for teaching me everything I need to know about America's old racial politics. Her motto, "Don't let other people's ignorance make you ignorant," daily keeps me from falling into the abyss of easy answers about racial matters.

To hip-hop generationers fighting this wrongheaded war in Iraq. In the words of Bob Marley, "Every day the bucket goes to the well. One day the bottom's gonna drop out." Hold your heads.

And to hip-hop activists on the battlefield to building a new world and a new politics. Your example is necessary, noted and the best gift we can give the next generation, other than change itself.

And

To the memory of Dr. Jacob Carruthers, whose example of "intellectual warfare" brought much beauty into the world; Lu Palmer, journalist, organizer and instigator extraordinaire, who knew the right combination of truth, insight and agitation "enough to make a Negro turn Black"; and "bridge generationer" Lisa Sullivan for teaching the hip-hop generation where to find our natural leaders.

No generation can choose the age or circumstance in which it is born, but through leadership it can choose to make the age in which it is born, an age of enlightenment, an age of jobs, and peace, and justice. Only leadership—that intangible combination of gifts, discipline, information, circumstance, courage, timing, will and divine inspiration—can lead us out of the crisis in which we find ourselves.

—Reverend Jesse Jackson, Democratic National Convention Address (San Francisco, July 18, 1984)

Contents

Preface

What goes around comes around I figure
Now we got white kids callin themselves "nigger."
—KRS-One "MC's Act Like They Don't Know"

The premise of this book is simple yet long overdue: the national conversation about race in this country has yet to catch up with the national reality. Given the technological gains of the past three decades, which ultimately defined the concept of the "information age," it's not far-fetched to assume that cutting-edge ideas in most areas of thought are quick to penetrate the mainstream. However, when it comes to racial matters, long an American obsession, the new reality of race is rarely part of the national conversation. Particularly ignored are the ideas and voices of the post–baby boom generation. Members of both generation X (those born between 1965 and 1984) and the millennium generation (those born between 1985 and

2004) have inherited and created a new world when it comes to living race in America. They are the first Americans to live their entire lives free of de facto segregation. This alone warrants our attention as we consider racial matters. What is more, today's acceptance of hip-hop as mainstream popular culture has radically altered the racial landscape. And in that nebulous space where hip-hop and popular culture meet, we see specific shifts in the ways young Americans are processing race. These shifts help explain the dawning of a new reality of race in America.

Hip-hop culture has its roots among young Blacks in urban communities throughout the northeastern United States. The Black subculture that emerged in the South Bronx in the early to mid-1970s began as what hip-hop pioneer Afrika Bambaataa called the five elements—graffiti art, break dancing, rapping, deejaying and "doing the knowledge." What is popularly known as hip-hop expanded beyond that definition by the early 1990s, mostly due to the commercialization of rap music. So today, when we speak of hip-hop culture, we are also referencing a hip-hop-specific language, body language, fashion, style, sensibility and worldview.

Part of the reason the culture is so influential among today's youth is that most young people who identify with hip-hop, unlike rock and roll and other musical genres, identify with more than music. Although bebop, the jazz subculture, was also associated with a cultural lifestyle, that lifestyle never ventured far beyond jazz aficionados. Hip-hop's emergence in a global information age is a major variable that sets it apart, vastly increasing its capacity to reach beyond anything the world has ever seen.

Throughout this book when the term "hip-hop" appears, depending on the context, I'm referring to either rap music or some other aspect of hip-hop culture. When I use it to describe individuals (e.g., hip-hop activists, hip-hop designers, hip-hop educators), I'm implying that they have a connection to the culture that goes beyond simply being pop culture consumers. When I use the term "mainstream hip-hop," I'm talking about aspects of the culture that have been packaged, often distorted and then sold by corporate America.

It is helpful to think of hip-hop's cultural movement as having both a local and a national manifestation. Even though hip-hop has reached a national consumer culture level, the local is still crucial to its survival. The local too, at times, has a life of its own. So it shouldn't be assumed that the local, off-the-radar manifestation of hip-hop is exclusively defined by what hip-hop does in the mainstream.

That American youth across race have embraced hip-hop culture, in both its local and national manifestations, is as much about hip-hop culture's sense of inclusiveness as it is a testament to American youth incorporating the founding fathers' "all men are created equal" rhetoric into their worldview. Another reason for its wide acceptance is that consumerism has become an American value. And hip-hop, as part of the American entertainment industry, is now for sale to all buyers.

But hip-hop music, no matter how widely accepted in the mainstream, isn't entertainment alone; it's also a voice of the voiceless. More than just a new genre of music, hip-hop since its inception has provided young Blacks a public platform in a society that previously rendered them mute. It has done the same for youth of other cultures as well. This in large measure explains hip-hop's mass appeal.

In the past decade American youth across the board have increasingly had to confront some of the economic and social frustrations (declining job options, deteriorating quality of education, rising incarceration for nonviolent crimes and the evaporation of living-wage employment) that began to handicap Black American youth in the early 1980s. A recent study (*Left Behind in the Labor Force*) by a team of scholars at Northeastern University found that by 2002, 5.5 million American young people between 16 and 24 were out of work, out of school and virtually dropping off the mainstream radar. At the same time white American youth, like their Latino American, Asian American and Native American counterparts, have embraced hip-hop culture. The music and culture of hip-hop, once deemed a Black thing, has been a ready refuge.

It is not only hip-hop's message of resistance to the status quo that young Americans find welcoming. The hip-hop cultural movement has provided a new arena of public space (although still largely off the radar of the mainstream) for young people to come together at local and national levels. In these spaces, which include local hip-hop collectives, spoken word venues, rap concerts and more, America's multicultural youth enjoy, observe and participate in this cultural arts movement.

A clear understanding of hip-hop's cross-cultural engagement, which may seem superficial to those outside the culture, affords us a unique lens for analyzing the evolution of ideas about race in America—changes that are manifesting themselves in a new generation. We are moving away from what I call the "old racial politics," characterized by adherence to stark differences—cultural, personal and political—between Black and white, away from cultural territorialism on both sides and away from an uncritical acceptance of stereotypes, also on both sides. The "new racial politics," on the other hand, is marked by nuance, complexity, the effects of commerce and commercialism and a sort of fluidity between cultures. The new views about race also allow us a radical standpoint from which to see the ways that America's outdated racial politics—a force more deeply embedded in our national psyche than we generally acknowledge—works against new definitions.

Although hip-hop is a refuge (albeit temporary) for many young people, old ideas about race continue to undermine attempts by pockets of youth to redefine the terms through hip-hop. Every day the nation clings to the old agenda and, even more troubling, rallies the younger generation to take up its dying causes. Examples are everywhere in pop culture, national debates and public policy at federal and state levels:

- In Al Sharpton's recent run for president a tired old racial history charade was played out. The campaign itself, and the way it was perceived in the media and political circles, took us back to the 1984 and 1988 presidential campaigns of Jesse Jackson, which were steeped in similar oppositional race politics. Was Sharpton's candidacy to be taken seriously or was he *just* a Black candidate?
- Affirmative action, seen in years past as a valuable tool for balancing racial inequalities, has itself recently been called racist. As it comes under attack at colleges and universities, the younger generation is strongly encouraged (if not coerced) to take up an older generation's dispute.
- Reparations is an issue with roots in the World War II generation. The manner in which the national discussion has been framed forces Americans to choose sides along outdated racial lines. One study at Harvard University, for

example, found that 90 percent of white Americans oppose reparations, while 90 percent of African Americans support it.

Old ways of thinking about race certainly persist in the younger generation. However, the mainstreaming of hip-hop culture has in part provided a space where American youth, Black and white included, can explore these new ideas together, even if the old racial politics are always lurking in the shadows.

This book attempts to unmask not only "the why" but "the who, what and when" of today's pop culture fascination: Why does hip-hop appeal to white youth? How is this generation's fascination with Black youth culture different from previous generations of American youth, given that R&B, jazz, blues and even rock and roll have all enjoyed similar cross-cultural mass appeal? What role do telecommunications, mass media and consumer culture play in these differences? What does generation X think about race? How do gen Xers differ on the issues from their parents and grandparents? How have ideas of race evolved? Are white kids stealing Black culture? Can culture exclusively belong to one race in the first place? Why is the race/color of hip-hop's audience so significant, and to whom? Where does America's racial politics fit into this phenomenon? Are young Americans achieving Martin Luther King Jr.'s dream via hip-hop?

A large part of this book's concern is hip-hop itself, especially the terrain of popular culture, youth culture, economics and politics, where Black and white kids interact. But at its core, *Why White Kids Love Hip-Hop* reveals the ways the younger generation is challenging the comfort zone that has made it fashionable for Americans to accept only baby steps in social change and race relations since the 1960s. This post–baby boom generation is forcing the country closer to Jefferson's assertion of equality: "We hold these truths to be self-evident, that all men are created equal." For the first time in forty years, a giant step in social change is before us.

Introduction

Toward a New Racial Politics

People are not born racist. Racism is learned behavior that is part of American culture. If hip-hop can change that, then there is reason for hope.
—Haki Madhubuti, author of *Run Toward Fear*

When most Americans, reared on a steady diet of American racial politics, think of white kids and hip-hop, two questions come to mind: (1) Will this generation's music, hip-hop, be appropriated by white America just as rock and roll was, leaving its Black originators all but forgotten? (2) If white youth are emulating the same young Black men our society has vilified for two centuries, are the pathologies and immoral behaviors deemed to be "Black problems" now going to infect the young whites who fall under the spell of hip-hop music and culture?

Our obsession with these questions leads us directly into the quagmire of America's outdated racial politics. Once there, exploring the new ground where white kids and hip-hop meet becomes nearly impossible. However, transcending the old racial politics is essential to discovering the new strategies this younger generation is evolving for working across historical divides like race, class and nationalism.

I have spent much of the past three years talking to white kids across the country who are engaging hip-hop on a variety of levels: from casual listeners who tune in to their local hip-hop radio station, to die-hard fans who attend the concert performance of their favorite rap stars, to actual hip-hop arts participants—deejays, break dancers, graffiti writers, emcees and spoken word poets. Some were teenagers, some college students, others were adults facing the challenges of children and other grown-up responsibilities. Here's what I found.

In response to the first question, hip-hop, as the mainstream pop culture of our time, has been appropriated by young white Americans. Still, in our visual age, no matter how mainstream hip-hop gets, it will never duplicate rock and roll's metamorphosis—becoming more strongly associated with white Americans than Blacks. In fact it would take an army of Eminems to divorce the image of hip-hop from young Black men, who after thirty years still dominate the art form.

To answer the second question, young whites are emulating Black cool—nothing new there. Talk long enough to almost any white kid into hip-hop, and he or she will openly acknowledge a fascination with Black culture. But it isn't just Black youth culture alone that American youth are consuming as they delve into hip-hop today. As elements of hip-hop culture have become absorbed into the American pop culture grab bag, hip-hop's mainstream packaging often includes elements of prison and street culture. Because of this morphing of cultures, now more than ever, it's often indistinguishable where hip-hop ends and prison and/or street culture begins. Parents, regardless of race, should be concerned about the various mixed messages transmitted to youth under the rubric of hip-hop.

However, white youth are not simply consuming pop culture messages wholesale, any more than Black kids are. Most hip-hop kids—white, Black, Latino, Asian and Native American—are taking from popular culture what they find useful, fashioning it to local needs, claiming it as their own and in the process placing their own stamp on it. This is happening regionally (whether East Coast, West Coast, Midwest or "dirty South") and internationally, as youth the world over are claiming hip-hop.

In writing *Why White Kids Love Hip-Hop*, I found it impossible to avoid answering the elementary questions demanded by America's old racial politics. I grapple with those issues and more in great detail in this book. However, the real value of this hip-hop generation to America lies beyond these hot-button racial issues. Questions like the one posed to me by Murray Foreman, hip-hop scholar and author of *The Hood Comes First: Race, Space and Place in Rap and Hip-Hop*, begin to take us to the territory: "The real test of white kids and hip-hop is what happens with police brutality when the white officers policing

Black and Latino communities are those same young whites who grew up on hip-hop?"

Foreman's question points to the way hip-hop (because of the way it treats race) is forcing aside the old racial politics. Over the past decade or so, as I've traversed the country documenting and engaging hip-hop, I've encountered other instances where the complexities of hip-hop as a mainstream American cultural phenomenon revealed its capacity to challenge the old racial politics, even as it sometimes reinforces them. There was the white hip-hop head in his early twenties who caused a ruckus at the hip-hop magazine where he worked as an editor. This young man was so immersed in hip-hop that he developed a predilection for the n-word. It rolled off his tongue as easily and frequently as it escapes the mouths of the young Blacks and Latinos with whom he daily discusses hip-hop. A twenty-something Black woman at the magazine, who grew up in an activist family, told him that his use of the word was offensive—even if the young Black men he talked to when peppering his conversation with the n-word didn't object. She demanded he not use the word in her presence.

There is the math teacher in his early sixties who doubles as a tennis coach at a prominent Midwestern public high school. Over the years, he's recognized the importance of hip-hop in the lives of today's youth and has tried in various ways to access hip-hop as a tool to reach students. He's even dabbled in hip-hop arts himself, penning countless lyrics and creating a rap alter ego that occasionally spits rhymes over the school intercom, an oddity, some would think, for a sixty-something white guy. The day his mostly white girls tennis team (on the return bus ride from an away match) sings along with a boom box playing Lil Jon and the Eastside Boyz' "Get Low," he contemplates retirement and reevaluates the extent to which the negative messages in hip-hop undermine its possibility for empowering students. "As powerful a medium as hip-hop is, why so much negativity," he asks me in frustration, not really expecting an answer.

At a liberal arts college in South Carolina, a young Black student leader, frustrated with Black students' negligible involvement in campus life, turns to hip-hop for answers. Like other casual observers throughout the country, she's seen advertisers, the fashion industry, educators and even Broadway turn to hip-hop. She plans Hip-Hop Day intending to use hip-hop to bolster student life. The turnout is tremendous—and all white.

A close-knit circle of housewives in the suburbs of Cleveland, all in their late twenties and early thirties, plan a girls night out—a three-hour drive to Detroit for a sold-out Eminem concert. "We spend our entire days trying to fit into a perfect little bubble," a thirty-three-year-old stay-at-home mom told me. "The perfect $500,000 houses. The perfect overscheduled kids. The perfect husbands. We love life, but we hate our lives. And so I think we identify more with hip-hop's passion, anger and frustration than we do this dream world."

Other moments bring pause. The heated debate at a planning committee meeting for a major hip-hop political event, where a young Black man storms out of the meeting after it was determined the event would be multicultural. He'd insisted that since hip-hop is a Black thing and whites have historically stolen Black culture, white involvement would water down the event. There was the episode on the television sitcom *Girl-friends*, where the white adopted sister of a Black woman accompanies her to the hair salon. The radio is playing Jay-Z's "H to the Izzo." All the women are singing along until the white sister joins in without skipping a beat, "I do this for my culture/to let em know what a nigga look like when a nigga's in a Rollsta." And finally, the often-heard critique of commercial hip-hop coming from white kids in the hip-hop underground that so-and-so white emcee is more hip-hop than 50 Cent or any other Black hip-hop artists topping the charts by nature of their being underground as opposed to commercial.

Complex spaces like these were my starting points to the larger inquiry. These and similar moments emerged as I interviewed numerous industry insiders and everyday fans about white kids and hip-hop. These are the difficult spaces that bring us face-to-face with any substantive exploration of white hip-hop kids. One of the most telling of these complexities came to light in an interview I conducted with an A&R at a major record label. "Right now, some of the hottest producers such as Alchemist and Scott Storch are white," he said, "and when you speak of the hip-hop underground, you are talking about a significant degree of white hip-hop kids." When I caught up with thirty-two-year-old Billy Wimsatt—author of *Bomb the Suburbs* (1994), one of the first critiques of white kids and hip-hop—we chopped it up about working across race in hip-hop's emerging political movement. He reiterated the A&R guy's point, placing it in a political context. "I'm horrified by the aspect of the white hip-hop thing where you can be a white hard-core underground hip-hop kid in, say, Minnesota, and not know a single Black person. Their whole social circle is white. Their favorite rappers are white, and they're trying to put out their own CDs, and so on. This is shockingly and violently decontextualized from what hip-hop came from and what it's about."

As I was nearing the end of this project, I met a young man named Matthew Nelkin who fit Wimsatt's description—kind of. Born and raised in Eugene, Oregon, he caught the hip-hop bug as a nine-year-old watching *Yo MTV Raps.* A few years later, he took odd jobs to earn money for deejay equipment. Oregon's population is around 90 percent white, and Eugene is equally homogeneous. Its Black population in the last census was less than 1,800 out of around 140,000 inhabitants. Yet during Matthew's formative years, Eugene had a fledgling hip-hop scene.

"I grew up as that white hip-hop kid where my immediate circle of friends was all white. At the same time, the hip-hop influences in and around Eugene were not all white. There was the radio stuff, a core group of talented and diverse local artists and crews who were out in the community making noise and lots of underground groups were coming in to do shows at venues that were selling out to mostly white audiences."

Matthew, now 25, says that growing up, he didn't think about the implications of being a white hip-hop kid. "It was all kind of innocent," he says, thinking back to when he was 15 and an aspiring deejay, collecting vinyl, making beats and hanging out at the community college radio station during the hip-hop show. "I loved hip-hop and worked to be a part of it. I remember one friend saying, 'Wow you guys are really good. Too bad you're not Black.' Before that, I never thought about the implications of being white and a part of hip-hop culture. At the time, I felt that he was misguided for saying that. As I've gotten older, I realize he recognized that hip-hop is Black culture and what he was saying is, 'This is Black culture, you're white and you're taking part of it.' It's a cognizant process that a lot of white kids into hip-hop don't admit to themselves."

Matthew's foray into hip-hop wasn't completely naive. He and his friends were aware that they were going against the grain. His reflections on how he felt as a young white kid into hip-hop suggest one of the ways hip-hop is forcing a new dialogue about race. "I went through a crisis after I read *Bomb the Suburbs* when I was 21," he says. "I thought about never being involved in hip-hop again. I thought it wasn't my place to do so. I went through months of being depressed. At the time, I was doing a hip-hop college radio show and I began to wonder if I was representing something that I didn't have the right to represent. I seriously thought about giving it up. I eventually asked myself the question, Who would want to deprive me of something that brought so much meaning to my life and that got me involved in positive things? To this day, I try to constantly check myself, bearing in mind what it means to be white, to have privilege in America and to take part in hip-hop. I attempt to be as responsible as possible. That's my compromise."

For every Matthew I met whose passion for hip-hop was more than a fad, there was an equal number of white kids whose fascination with hip-hop went no further than a desire to learn the latest Usher dance moves. Matthew and those like him, on the other hand, are engaging hip-hop on a deeper, cerebral level. Theirs is a constant struggle not only to absorb the art, politics and cultural roots of hip-hop but to make sense of its significance in their lives.

"When I was in high school," Matthew tells me, "a friend came up to me one day and told me that he had been writing rhymes for about a year, but was afraid to tell anyone. It was normal for that to happen back then. We still got made fun of by some of our friends for being white and into hip-hop. Looking back on my formative years, I see that we were trying to create an identity for ourselves that was more substantive than what we were handed in public school, church or any other outlet. We were really fighting for our spirits, fighting to define ourselves outside of mainstream American society by latching onto an oppositional identity and the perceived power in hip-hop."

His observations illuminate what's really at stake as white kids delve into hip-hop. Our country stands at a crucial crossroads. The true story of America in the post-1970s era is the tale of how we as a nation have abandoned our young. We're not placing great enough emphasis on educating or listening to the voices of American youth. Our public schools and quality of life for a significant number of our young are in serious decline. Additionally, in our lifetime, jobs for our youth have diminished in quality and quantity. Instead of rising to the challenge as a nation, we're more focused on placating corporate elites (can you say Haliburton?). Equally disturbing, we've returned to two irritants that helped spark the revolution that brought the country into existence two hundred years ago: taxation without representation and a greater concern with what's going on outside of the country (Iraq, Iran, Korea, Syria and Cuba, for starters) than what's going on inside it. Humankind has been here before. America, like the great empires before her, may be displaying the early warning signs of decline. The one hope of saving the country could be simply listening to our young people. Rather than the source of the problems facing American youth, hip-hop, more than anything else, has helped prepare our youth to confront not only race but some of the crises facing the nation's young people.

As I write this, I've just returned from Milan, Italy, where I met with a group of mostly white activists who asked me about hip-hop's political forays and its potential to affect the future of America and the world. I tell them what I believe: that hip-hop has been the response to the reckless abandonment of young people in this country. I point out that the primary solutions our government has offered for youth problems facing this generation have been incarceration and medication—an escalation of incarceration rates between 1970 to 2000 (from 200,000 to over 2 million) alongside an escalating tendency to medicate school-age youth, as prescriptions for psychiatric drugs in this age group nearly tripled from 1996 to 2003. Ironically, as the economic structure at the heart of these problems is the same monster giving hip-hop's cultural movement its wings, there is still reason for hope.

As young people worldwide gravitate to hip-hop and adapt it to their local needs, responding to the crises of our time, they are becoming equipped with a culture that corporate and political elites can't control. It's a youth-centered culture that is self-motivating and only requires its participants to have a mouth, the ability to listen and frustration with business as usual. This cultural movement is currently making way for hip-hop's emerging political movement. Given the way the culture is being absorbed by young people around the globe, these movements may be the catalysts necessary to jump-start an international human rights movement in this generation, a movement with the potential to parallel if not surpass yesterday's civil rights successes. *Why White Kids Love Hip-Hop* is an attempt to shine a light on the possibilities.

PART ONE

Questions
Do White Boys Want to Be Black?

A little over a year ago, Bill O'Reilly, the conservative talk show host who does more than anyone else to keep hip-hop in the news, had *American Idol* host Simon Cowell as a guest on his show, the *O'Reilly Factor*. After asking Cowell a series of questions about the music industry and its stars, O'Reilly turned to his favorite whipping boy, hip-hop. He drew a firm line between Elvis Presley's shocking dance moves and hip-hop's bad boy purveyors of so-called gangsta rap. Wiggling provocatively and singing about love, in the world according to O'Reilly, is vastly different from rapping about the gritty hip-hop underworld of sex, drugs and violence. Since O'Reilly had taken this position on hip-hop many times before, it was business as usual. The turning point came when Cowell, in his response, referred to Eminem as a genius.

O'Reilly asked him why. Cowell answered, "He's somebody who understood that white boys want to be Black and exploited that fact."

As much as I relished seeing O'Reilly stunned and set back on his heels in a discussion of hip-hop, I disagreed with Cowell. White boys don't necessarily want to be Black. This conclusion is an oversimplification. Donald Trump used a similar line of reasoning a decade ago in an interview on *NBC News*. He said that if he could choose, he'd be young and Black and male.*

A well-educated Black man has a tremendous advantage over a well-educated white in terms of the job market. And I think sometimes a Black may think they don't really have the advantage . . . but I've said on occasion—even about myself—if I were starting off today, I would love to be a well-educated Black because I really believe they do have an actual advantage today.

A cursory glance at the statistics regarding Black men, in regard to college graduation rates, unemployment rates, wealth, incarceration, health and life expectancy, makes it clear that being young, Black and male is hardly advantageous. And

---

*More recently Trump weighed in with another preposterous claim that he would no longer hire men because the women in the early episodes of his reality show *The Apprentice* were showing more business savvy. As with the statement regarding Black men, Trump takes the word "patronizing" to a whole new level.

although hip-hop has, in the past half century, helped frame an extra-sexy multicultural space, it's hardly more attractive than the space young white males enjoy in American culture. At the same time, hip-hop's cultural movement has helped equate "Black" with "cool" for another generation of white Americans.* In this sense, Cowell is on to something. As a Brit, he feels comfortable acknowledging something white American baby boomers like O'Reilly won't—that despite the ways African American men have been vilified during this younger generation's lifetime, more and more young whites are abandoning old apprehensions about young Blacks and openly embracing Black youth culture.

Yes, a white kid engaging in the predominantly Black medium of hip-hop is going to be deemed cool by his peers—if he can pull it off, especially in a climate where hip-hop is mainstream youth culture. By doing so, however, that kid is not choosing race suicide. Eminem is not seeking to become Black and abandon whiteness. Instead, his being white is what makes him so attractive to the marketplace. Or as Lisa Scott, director of social equity at Pennsylvania's Bloomsburg University, pointed out to me in an informal discussion with a handful of Black intellectuals on the topic of white kids and hip-hop on a blistering cold Martin Luther King Day 2003, "Part of what Eminem is selling is whiteness."

---

*See MEE Productions 1992 report, *Reaching the Hip-Hop Generation.*

1

Why White Kids Love Hip-Hop

First of all music is something you just feel. Period. And with hip-hop it's like a movie. You get to put on this pair of headphones, close your eyes and go through this movie without experiencing it for the most part. You get to go through this fantasy world, where the ultra, super hero guy who nobody could harm, has been through a tough situation and he came out great. Take the CD out. Take the headphones off and go shoot hoops. That's a very easy education.

—Hip-hop mogul and rapper Jay-Z

For the past five years Jeremy Miller has made the thirty-minute commute from suburban New Jersey to his Manhattan office. The chief operating officer of *The Source*, a pioneering publication that for over a decade has been the bible of hip-hop, Jeremy has been involved in the magazine in various capacities for thirteen years. His commute takes him through the full range of America's socioeconomic backgrounds; from affluent suburban neighborhoods and upscale cookie-cutter developments like Colonia and Edison, through solidly middle-class communities like Woodbridge, and to blue-collar townships like Linden and Rahway to the grittier neighborhoods of Newark, where on any given day he's a drive-by observer to homelessness, prostitution and other signposts of America's forgotten poverty.

Besides this downward socioeconomic spiral, Jeremy is keenly aware of the presence of hip-hop culture—whether it's white kids posing on the stoops in low-income hoods or the occasional Suburban with 20s, full of white boys wearing skullies and shades and pumping Jay-Z.

"That's the evolution of hip-hop," he says. "It's spread out to the suburbs."

With young whites now comprising a sizable audience for hip-hop music, this evolution of hip-hop makes many politicians, mainsteam commentators and parents uncomfortable. They correctly identify hip-hop as a Black youth subculture that many young whites are enthusiastically engaging. Uncritically accepted, however, are the accompanying pop culture perceptions of young Black males as criminals and young Black women as "bitches," "hos," "chickenheads" and worse. Over the past decade, as we've witnessed the rise of conservatism in America, this dissatisfaction has found a public voice in the claim that American morality is disintegrating and hip-hop's arrival as a mainstream cultural phenomenon is a large part of the problem. Put bluntly, too many white kids are trying to be Black. Hip-hop, these critics say, is nothing more than a form of vulgar self-degradation that is corrupting young white Americans. These self-appointed defenders of American morality fail to see that hip-hop is much more than pop culture. Instead of corrupting young whites, hip-hop is helping usher in a new racial politics that has come into its own with the post–baby boom generation.

Hip-Hop and American Morality

A brief history of this anti–hip-hop crusade is in order. In the summer of 2003 during the Democratic presidential primary race, Staten Island city councilman James Oddo launched into a tirade about graffiti. Oddo declared his disapproval of the decision by Democratic presidential candidate Howard Dean to commission Keo, a graffiti artist, to create a mural for a campaign stop in Manhattan's Bryant Park. Dean's team wanted a concept that would appeal to youth and recognized hip-hop as central in today's American youth culture. The councilman felt this was an insult to the city of New York. "Maybe in your world, graffiti vandals are artists," Oddo said in a letter to Dean immediately following the appearance. "In New York City, and in the real world, they are criminals who destroy our quality of life." In Oddo's world, graffiti, the visual art component of hip-hop culture, was a step into the barbarized underworld of Black youth culture—not something to be exalted at a traditional, high-profile political rally. It's a message that hasn't gone away. Despite hip-hop's pervasive presence in American life, it is still the scapegoat for declining American values.

The same was true over a decade earlier in 1992, when Vice President Dan Quayle remarked about rapper Tupac Shakur and hip-hop: "This music has no place in our society." Quayle's comments came on the heels of the murder of a Texas state trooper. Investigators claimed to have found a tape of Tupac's "2Pacalypse Now" inside the accused shooter's car. Although later news reports revealed that no such tape was found, Quayle didn't hesitate to draw the line between violence and hip-hop. As much as he was concerned about American morality, he was also interested in laying the groundwork for George H. W. Bush's reelection campaign. Later, during the campaign, he and the president went on to connect media giant Time Warner, specifically its hip-hop artists like Ice-T, with a decline in national decency.

Two years later former education secretary Bill Bennett, author of the best-selling *The Book of Virtues*, helped renew the crusade to clean up what he called "the filth" of the entertainment industry. Young Blacks were again in the eye of the storm. Although Bennett spoke broadly of pop culture as the problem, his poster boys were Black. Rap artists like Tupac, Dr. Dre and Snoop Dogg were his targets in 1995, when he set his crosshairs on record companies Interscope and Time Warner for their complicity in elevating Black youth culture into the mainstream. Again, in not-so-coded language, it was hip-hop that was sullying the pure and white moral values of American youth. "If you look at some rap videos, they're barbarous," Bennett declared in an interview with *Newsweek* magazine in 1994. "We know what happens to children with a steady diet of this sort of thing, particularly when they aren't offered—as an alternative—things good, positive and uplifting. We've seen a phenomenal increase in social pathologies, crime, broken families and so on. There are a lot of things going on here, but to me one of them is a culture that's become increasingly trashy."

This fear-of-a-Black-planet line of thinking wasn't the exclusive domain of conservative race baiters. Bill Bennett received a helping hand from Democratic Senators Joe Lieberman (Connecticut) and Sam Nunn (Georgia) when they joined him a year later in targeting record labels that produced so-called gangsta rappers.

Democrats weren't new to this game. Never one to be upstaged by Republicans, Bill Clinton had much earlier taken his cue from his opponents' campaign playbook and went for the jugular. On the campaign trail in June 1992, Clinton spoke at an Operation PUSH/Rainbow Coalition event, invited by Jesse Jackson. He took the organization to task for inviting raptivist Sista Souljah to speak there the previous night, accusing her of spreading a "message of hate."

Slick Willie's verbal pimp-slapping of Sista Souljah in the presence of Black leaders (many of whom would later have his back during the Monica Lewinsky scandal) should forever be recognized for what it was: a signal to Blacks that their vote was securely in the hip pocket of the Democrats (*hell, they have no where else to go,* according to the conventional "wisdom"). Clinton, chosen by the Democratic Leadership Committee, had to let right-leaning Democrats (and some centrist Republicans) know that regardless of how much love Blacks had for him, he would ride for right interests first and foremost. Equally important, Clinton had to make it plain that the views espoused by young Blacks, even highly educated Blacks like Sista Souljah,

were no more welcome on America's moral menu than the grittiest words of so-called gangsta rappers. In fact, they would be
treated as one and the same. Clinton's commentary, more than a
response to Sista Souljah, was a message to all that his access and
close proximity to Blacks afforded him authority in the Black
community. He didn't have to whine and point fingers, like
Dole, Quayle or Bennett. Instead, his tactic was direct, hands-on
confrontation with old guard and emerging Black leaders, insulting them and giving up the tough love at the same time. It
was a message that resonated throughout his presidency relative
to Blacks and persists on the left and the right in the post-
Clinton era. At that event in 1992, Clinton played an in-your-
face race card that his colleagues on the right could never dream
up: likening Souljah to then Ku Klux Klan leader David Duke.

And then along came Fox News Channel and the *O'Reilly
Factor*. Bill O'Reilly's precise dissection of hip-hop earned him
the tongue-in-cheek 2002 award Dopest MC of the Year from
hip-hop commentator Davey D, who concluded that, when it
comes to attacking hip-hop artists, "he hasn't lost a battle."
Whether lambasting Pepsi for choosing the rapper Ludacris as
its spokesman, condemning Snoop Dogg for peddling *Girls
Gone Wild* videos (and allegedly forcing underage girls to appear in them), blaming the hip-hop lifestyle for what he called
the "assassination" of rappers like Jam Master Jay or beating up
on a Midwestern high school's decision to allow Jay-Z to be
principal for a day, O'Reilly has been unrelenting in his assault
on hip-hop. And it doesn't matter whether he's chopping it up
with *Source* founder Dave Mays, godfather of hip-hop Russell
Simmons or the rap trailblazer turned minister Rev Run, his po-

sition doesn't change. Anything positive hip-hop might bring to the table is dismissed wholesale. What matters is that rap is bad for America's children: "For years, I've been saying that the antisocial lyrics contained in many rap songs and the overall tone of boorish behavior in the hip-hop world is having a destructive influence on many of America's most at-risk children," O'Reilly said on the *O'Reilly Factor* on May 30, 2001, touting a standard refrain that he would regurgitate time after time in coming years.

The tendency of critics to reduce white kids' fascination with hip-hop to the old racial politics formula keep from national view an emerging chapter in America's racial history. A new racial politics has been unfolding in the post–baby boom generation that before now has not been adequately discussed. Five primary variables helped created the climate for this new racial politics to emerge: the rise of the global economy and a resulting sense of alienation among young whites in the 1980s and 1990s; significant ruptures in the popular music scene; a further shifting American economy at the turn of the millennium, which was accompanied by a declining sense of white privilege; the institutionalization of key aspects of the civil rights movement; and finally the sociopolitical range of post-1960s Black popular culture. Examined collectively, these variables begin to construct a picture of the new racial politics.

The Global Economy and Alienation (the 1980s)

First and foremost among the reasons white kids love hip-hop is the growing sense of alienation from mainstream American life they experienced in the 1980s. As the 1970s turned into the 1980s and America moved into what was billed as a new economy, Americans, regardless of race and class, began to feel increasingly uncertain. For African Americans, specifically hip-hop generationers (those born between 1965 and 1984), this economic shift made itself felt in the now well-documented underground economy, crack cocaine wars, paramilitary policing units and their aftermath; the busting-at-the-seams American prison system. The generation of white kids in the same age-group, dubbed generation X, was confronted by socioeconomic issues that alienated them from the mainstream as well. Although the employment prospects facing young whites entering the job force in the 1980s and 1990s were not as bleak as those facing their Black and Latino counterparts, those in the middle and working classes faced slimmer prospects than their parents' generation had. During this period, wages continued to fall for unskilled workers, regardless of race, and the ranks of the poor expanded. Meanwhile, the superrich got richer. Seventy percent of gains in family income went to the wealthiest 1 percent of Americans in the decade between the late 1970s and the late 1980s, according to economic data compiled by the Federal Reserve. This period was also marked by longer workdays for parents and inevitably less family time. By the mid-1980s, young whites' sense of alienation intensified even though Blacks were to some degree a buffer (as in, "things are bad but worse on the other side of the fence"). Blacks' unemployment rates, for example, remained at least twice that of their white counterparts throughout the 1980s and much of the 1990s.

One of the more significant signs of growing dissatisfaction among the American middle class was the rise in prescription drug use for depression and anxiety among youth. According to Children and Adults with Attention Deficit/Hyperactivity Disorder (CHADD), a national nonprofit organization based in Landover, Maryland, the number of American children being treated with psychiatric drugs tripled between 1987 and 1996. Over the past two decades, behavioral drugs like Ritalin and Luvox have increasingly been prescribed to middle- and upper-middle-class schoolchildren. Some researchers suggest that these students more often attend schools where parents want their children to have an edge. They argue that teachers promote the use of prescriptions for attention deficit and hyperactive disorders (ADHD) to help them keep control of the classroom and disruptive students. By 1999, more than 2.5 million U.S. children were taking these drugs. Experts say these rising numbers are in part the result of research on how the brain functions, which exploded during the 1980s and 1990s. At the same time, prescription use across the board is at an all-time high. Critics, including Dr. Peter Breggin, director of the International Center for the Study of Psychiatry and Psychology, a nonprofit research organization in Bethesda, Maryland, argue that doctors are overprescribing such drugs. Prozac sales are currently estimated at about $2 billion, Zoloft around $1.4 billion and Paxil just under $1 billion annually. Whereas 900,000 children were using Ritalin in 1990, for example, 5 million children were being prescribed the drug in 2000. According to the Agency for Healthcare Research and Quality, prescriptions of stimulants and antidepressant drugs to treat ADHD in children and adolescents doubled between 1996 and 1999.

A Changing Pop Music Scene (the 1990s)

It was during this period of rising alienation that the first wave of young whites were drawn to hip-hop, some as early as the mid-1980s and rising by the early 1990s. Unlike many white kids who are part of hip-hop's consumer audience today, young white Americans who began identifying with hip-hop during the mid-1980s for the most part were not in it for the arts alone. Many viewed hip-hop as an appealing antiestablishment culture. Hip-hop was still primarily an underground phenomenon. Even those hip-hop records that began to break through to a national audience only enjoyed moderate sales (at best going gold) in comparison to today's routine multiplatinum sellers. Another characteristic of the earliest wave of young white hip-hop kids was their political orientation. Some had left-leaning tendencies or at least sympathized with Black issues, whereas in the current climate hip-hop is mainstream pop culture and being immersed in Black culture or even having Black friends is not a prerequisite. And in those days, for most white hip-hop kids, including those outside the New York City metropolitan area—areas where hip-hop as a culture in its entirety had not yet arrived—hip-hop music, contrary to popular opinion, was more than a mainstream "cultural safari" ride.

"When hip-hop made its way out west," says California native Kyle Stewart, 41, who grew up in the 1980s with punk rock music, "I made what I felt was a natural progression into hip-hop. Like punk, hip-hop was counterculture. It gave youth a voice to tell the truth and exposed the ills of society, especially racism and our hypocritical government. Also, the beats were infectious."

The more progressive and radical messages of Public Enemy, Poor Righteous Teachers, X-Clan and KRS-One attracted young whites like Kyle. So did the idea of Black kids having voice and agency. Hip-hop's innate inclusiveness also made it attractive. For many white kids who got into hip-hop during this period, being down with hip-hop was as much a political statement as it was an alternative musical choice.

"I believe there was a point in time, before hip-hop became mainstream, that embracing hip-hop culture in itself was a form of activism," continues Stewart, who's been involved in a variety of activist efforts over the past two decades and recently cofounded the League of Pissed Off Voters. "To me, hip-hop is ultimately about self-determination, so to embrace it, especially back in the '80s, was making a social statement." This sentiment is a recurring one among white hip-hop kids who caught the hip-hop bug in that earlier wave.

By the late 1980s, a sense of alienation specific to generation X was gaining expression in grunge music, a Seattle-inspired fusion of rock and punk that captured a huge following of young white kids. Many identified with the dark angst of a handful of bands, like Green River, Sound Garden, Alice in Chains, Mudhoney and Smashing Pumpkins, which personified the movement. All captured the sense of teen angst that hadn't existed in rock for years. More than any one musical moment for American youth coming of age in the 1980s and

1990s, grunge restored rock music as the voice of American youth rebellion, something that characterized earlier eras of rock and roll. Groups like Nirvana and Pearl Jam helped take a marginal music from the underground to mainstream youth culture. By 1991, from major radio stations to MTV, grunge was the order of the day. To date, Pearl Jam's album *Ten* holds the record of the most units sold for a debut album in music history (12 times platinum). Unfortunately for a generation in need of a cultural movement to call its own, by 1995, less than a decade after it gained national appeal, grunge had reached its peak and had begun to taper off. Many point to the suicide of Nirvana's Kurt Cobain as the beginning of the end of grunge's reign as a major cultural force. Around the same time grunge began to fall off, countless white kids, joining their African American and Latino counterparts, began to identify more strongly with hip-hop's cadence. For the first time hip-hop began to claim significant numbers of white kids among its audience.

Every cultural movement needs its propagandists. The *Source*, which came on the scene in 1988 as a one-page newsletter, played that role for hip-hop. It appealed to the lifestyle of hip-hop rather than simply reporting on the music and entertainment aspects. Kids who wanted to understand more about the lifeblood that fueled the music that was fast becoming mainstream American culture turned to *The Source* and later other publications like *Rap Pages*, *Rap Sheet*, *XXL* and *Vibe*. Not until the mid- to late-1990s would mainstream print media begin to provide serious, accurate coverage of the hip-hop world. Before that, it was up to hip-hop's propaganda arm to dissect the intricacies of hip-hop culture—delving into the business, artists' tastes and more. Efforts like these helped grow hip-hop beyond the musical product and gave young whites far removed from urban settings a means of discovering nearly anything they wanted to know about Black youth culture and the artists spearheading this cultural awakening.

Around this time, with the nation focused on the O.J. Simpson murder trial, the Oklahoma City bombing, the Republican takeover of Congress for the first time in forty years and the Million Man March, the country was once again polarized around race. Also during the mid-1990s, the hip-hop world was under the spell of the Notorious B.I.G. and Tupac Shakur. Puff Daddy, the former wonder boy of Uptown Records, realized that B.I.G. had the right stuff to catapult his newly formed Bad Boy label into the stratosphere. Hip-hop's legendary strongman Suge Knight had already enjoyed tremendous success by partnering with Interscope and had further strengthened his reputation as one of hip-hop's major players by bailing Tupac Shakur out of an upstate New York prison, for $1.4 million. Six days after he was released, Pac told the *Los Angeles Times* (October 29, 1995), "I've been in the studio every waking hour since I got out. . . . You're going to feel the entire 9 months of what I went through on this album. I'm venting my anger."

Tupac and B.I.G. had seemingly overnight become the biggest names in hip-hop. Their fame soon overshadowed Snoop Dogg (whose public persona was still suffering from his murder trial) and Dr. Dre (who was in the midst of parting company with Suge Knight). To give some perspective on the importance of Tupac and B.I.G. in the hip-hop world at this time, consider that Nas, who would later vie for prominence as hip-hop's king of New York (following the deaths of Pac and

B.I.G. in 1996 and 1997), was missing in action between his aliases Nas Escobar and God's Son. Big name rappers like DMX, Jay-Z and 50 Cent had yet to break through from the obscurity of hip-hop's underground. And Eminem, the so-called Elvis of hip-hop, wasn't even registering on the national radar.

The release of B.I.G.'s *Ready to Die* and Tupac's two-volume CD *All Eyes on Me* almost singlehandedly helped establish hip-hop as a staple of American culture. They would go on to become two of hip-hop's most popular and best-selling artists of all time. But it was their public feud, couched in what the media called "the East Coast/West Coast war," that made it nearly impossible for anyone—neither young whites nor their baby boomer parents—to ignore hip-hop.

Like those who had identified with hip-hop about a decade earlier, many young whites who fell in love with hip-hop around this time identify hip-hop's creative, engaging music as their initial attraction. Jeremy Miller told me, "I think there is still something about the music that if you get it, it doesn't get any better. In terms of the beats, the way the words are put over the music, it's just powerful music to me and I think the white kids into it now really feel the power in the music in the way it's put together."

Most found in it something original and distinctive that spoke to the time, a music with a message that distinguished it from the pop music pack. More than any other music, hip-hop remains tailor-made to the here and now. In a quick-fix, fast-paced, global culture, hip-hop incorporates fluid elements (music, language, nuance) at lightening speed while remaining easily accessible across cultures.

As young Americans, Black and white, accepted hip-hop as their own, hip-hop CD sales set one record after another. By 1998, when rapper Lauryn Hill won five Grammy Awards for her album *The Miseducation of Lauryn Hill*, hip-hop had already begun to gain regular coverage in mainstream newspapers like the *New York Times*, *Washington Post* and *Boston Globe*—whereas previously hip-hop's mainstream press coverage was mostly a negative affair. Elite magazines like *Vanity Fair*, *New Yorker* and *GQ* and television programs like *60 Minutes* and *Nightline* also realized they could no longer ignore hip-hop as a news story. Over time, feature stories and commentary on hip-hop in these publications became more numerous and gained greater accuracy. So pervasive was hip-hop's mainstream presence that in a postgrunge era, hip-hop even began influencing rock bands. In this way, hip-hop led to the creation of a whole new subgenre, dubbed rock-rap hybrids—Kid Rock, Rage Against the Machine, Korn, and others.

The Economy and White Privilege (2000 and Beyond)

With the arrival of the 1990s, the U.S. economy enjoyed its longest economic expansion in history. Still, the economic situation for the vast majority in the middle was in flux. Whereas working-class jobs provided access to a middle-class lifestyle for our parents' generation, the job prospects for working-class generation Xers, by comparison, were grim. The upper-middle-class lifestyle that news media, entertainment and government sold daily as what it meant to be American remained unattainable for most. Education, which had been the fastest way out of poverty for previous generations, was no longer the great equalizer. Rising college costs far outdistanced inflation, making the cost of a college education prohibitive for even middle-class Americans. The trend of parents working longer hours to make ends meet and to secure the redefined and ever-illusive American Dream continued. A more stressed, fragile family unit was the order of the day. Government seemed more a tool for the rich and superrich than one of, for and by the people. An America that promised so much was delivering less and less to average Americans.

The close of the century brought with it the bursting of the dot-com bubble at the end of the 1990s. The recession that began in March 2001 was accompanied by an intensified sense of white middle-class alienation from the mainstream as trends like exporting manufacturing jobs and outsourcing white-collar jobs overseas continued. Between 2001 and mid-2003, the United States lost around 2.7 million jobs, the worst net job loss in two decades. Two million of those were manufacturing jobs. According to the Association of Manufacturers, every state lost manufacturing jobs during this period. In New York, for example, half the jobs lost were in manufacturing.

The gap between rich and poor Americans widened between 1979 and 2000, according to a 2003 Congressional Budget Office report. This report also found that 2000 was the year of greatest economic disparity between rich and poor Americans since 1979. In 2000, the top 1 percent of American taxpayers (2.8 million Americans) earned $862,700 after taxes, compared to the bottom 40 percent (110 million Americans), whose after-tax income was $21,118. At the same time, according to the Census Bureau, the number of Americans living in poverty increased by 3 million between the beginning of 2001 and the end of 2002. The Census Bureau also reported a 1.8 percent decline in per capita income as well as a 1.1 percent drop in median household income for 2002. For 2003, the Census Bureau reported an additional 1.3 million Americans in poverty. All of these statistics indicate some of the hardest economic changes middle-class Americans had experienced in nearly a century. Other notable statistics and reports point to a continuing economic shift:

- Although those with college degrees on average earn 50 percent more than those without, the cost of a college education is increasingly prohibitive. According to the American Council of Education, hundreds of colleges and universities have been raising tuition costs faster than inflation. According to the annual survey of the College Board, in 2003, college tuition showed the highest increase in twenty-five years. Among private schools, tuition increased by 6 percent. At public four-year colleges, tuition increased by 14 percent. The same was true for community colleges that year. For 2004, tuition increased by 10.5 percent for four-year public schools, 6 percent at private schools and 9 percent at community colleges.
- According to the National Low-Income Housing Coalition, rising housing costs have outpaced wages. A study entitled *Out of Reach in 2003* found that in most states,

workers need to earn twice the federal minimum wage (which was last increased to $5.15/hr. in 1997) in order to afford decent housing.

- The number of Americans lacking health insurance increased every year from 1987 to 1998, according to the Census Bureau. The figure jumped again in 2002 (though it did not go as high as in 1998), as the number of employers sponsoring coverage decreased by 1.3 million. Just over 15 percent of the population, or 45 million people, were without health insurance coverage in 2003.

- According to the Bureau of Labor Statistics, dual-income families radically increased between the 1960s and the turn of the century. In 1995, 60 percent of married couples were dual-career couples, up from 44 percent in 1967. In 1996, 62 percent of all mothers with children under 6 were in the labor force, up from 39 percent in 1975.

- Americans also increased their debt. According to a 2002 study by Demos, *Borrowing to Make Ends Meet: The Growth of Credit Card Debt in the 1990s,* American families on average experienced a 53 percent increase in credit card debt, from $2,697 in 1989 to $4,126 in 2001, tripling overall American credit card debt from $238 billion to $692 billion. Between 1980 and 2003, personal bankruptcy filings tripled, according to a February 2005 report from the Center for American Progress.

As if the economic shifts were not enough, the growth of the "minority" population may further heighten white Americans' anxiety. Given the growing visibility of successful people of color, white Americans sense now more than ever that they have to compete with America's other racial and ethnic groups. The decline of white privilege has intensified as whites observe Blacks and other American people of color succeeding beyond the entertainment world as educators, in countless positions of authority in corporate America and in local, state and federal government.* Black success in the entertainment world, for that matter, has gone beyond anything ever before relative to white America in terms of salaries and influence. As the future of white privilege is challenged, white Americans, young and old, increasingly feel a sense of uncertainty about their present and future.

Abroad this uncertainty can be measured by an increasing awareness that the Western world can't continue to ignore past and current exploitation around the globe. "This is a central reason why the Bush administration pulled out of Durban," Becky Thompson told me. Thompson, who's white and the author of *A Promise and a Way of Life: White Anti-Racist Activism* (2001), was referring to the United Nations World Conference Against Racism held in South Africa in 2001. "They saw that the reparations issue was an international one and that people of color all over the world are holding white people and the industrial world accountable for colonialism. White people know we have blood on our hands. As the demographics shift, whites are increasingly afraid that the day is coming when we will have to be accountable." Likewise at home.

The most recent responses to this sense of alienation haven't been uniform or predictable. For some older and

---

*This is a perception issue, since whites still far outdistance Blacks in salaries, wealth, access and so on.

younger Americans alike, this gets channeled into nostalgic calls for a return to the good old days of 1950s America. There are those World War II tomes about the "greatest generation," alongside the outspoken right-wing political agendas of politicians like Trent Lott and Strom Thurmond, not to mention the more sexily packaged messages of the neoconservatives like Newt Gingrich and Ann Coulter. All advocate a return to the 1950s as a strategy for achieving a better America today. And for an extremely small minority, there are the obscure white supremacist factions such as the Aryan Nation and the National Alliance, which continue to enjoy a following.

Significant numbers of white youth channel this intensifying sense of alienation into a fascination with hip-hop. Some are drawn to hip-hop's escapist messages. Some are caught up in the contemporary climate of pop culture that makes hip-hop the flavor of the month. Still others feel the same sense of disenfranchisement as other dispossessed Americans, Black and otherwise. Most recognize that government has increasingly abandoned the interests of working-class people and is aligned almost exclusively with the interests of the rich and superrich.

Institutionalizing Civil Rights Culture

The globalization of the economy, a changing pop music scene and a declining sense of white privilege were all factors in the rise of white youth obsession with hip-hop, but there were others. A fourth societal change that paved the way for white American youth's engagement with hip-hop was the institutionalization of aspects of the civil rights movement's ideology. In the years since the assassination of Martin Luther King Jr., his philosophy of inclusion has worked its way into mainstream American folklore and national culture. From the creation of the national holiday honoring him in 1983 to the incorporation of the history of the civil rights movement into elementary and high school curriculums and college classrooms, the idea of inclusion has became a central part of American national culture and identity. The implications of this are especially profound for those who have lived their entire lives in the postsegregation era. By 1996, civil rights rhetoric was ever being adopted by politicians on both the left and the right. That year, a California Republican Party advertising campaign used a video excerpt from King's "I Have a Dream" speech in a television advertisement.*

This repositioning of African American culture as a cornerstone of American identity, specifically connecting the civil rights movement to America's ideal of freedom and justice for all, raised national awareness of Black American culture, at least superficially. In essence, our collective understanding of the civil rights movement serves as a gateway to a more enlightened national discussion of race. The 1977 television film *Roots* and the PBS broadcast of the first six segments of the documentary *Eyes on the Prize* in 1987 further broadened that awareness. By the mid-1990s, the increasing recognition and

---

*The ad supported Proposition 209, which called for banning affirmative action programs. The King family protested the ad, saying it was an attempt to suggest that MLK didn't support affirmative action.

celebration of Black History Month and the African American holiday Kwanzaa in educational settings heightened national familiarity with Black culture. Kwanzaa, for example, was primarily observed by Black cultural nationalists in the early 1970s, but by the 1990s had made its way into mainstream media, classrooms and community celebrations. By 1997 the U.S. Postal Service issued the first stamp honoring the holiday. (Another followed in 2004.)

This new reality influenced the degree to which white youth have engaged hip-hop. The narratives of the civil rights movement in history textbooks, the telling and retelling of the same in documentaries and feature films, the endless replaying of audio and video footage of King's speeches on radio and television year after year (following the establishment of the King holiday and strong pockets of resistance to it) have all helped familiarize white kids with distant or unknown aspects of Black culture. For the first time, most young white Americans came of age with a fair degree of awareness of African American culture. At the same time, public acceptance of old stereotypical assumptions was diminishing.

All of this was reinforced by the Afrocentric movement of the early 1990s, a holdover of late 1960s and early 1970s Black cultural nationalism both in the academy and on the street. Molefi Asante's pioneering African American Studies Ph.D. program at Temple University (formed in 1987), along with the public debates between Black scholars like Leonard Jeffries and defenders of the traditional canon, routinely made headlines. X-cap mania, kente cloth–patterned graduation sashes, bow ties, cummerbunds and even umbrellas were the most visible signs of the street manifestation. Bookstores that called themselves Afrocentric, barbershops, hairstyles, music and even churches suggest that its influence cut across class lines.

"It manifested itself as a cultural style in everything from clothing to how people greet each other to some extent to how we think about family, community and rituals," says Manning Marable, director of the Institute for African American Research at Columbia University, of the popular version of Afrocentricity. "Afrocentricism, the popular version, reflected a kind of identification with Blackness, cultural solidarity with people of African descent at home and abroad. And in that sense it became popularized to the point of common sense within most predominantly Black communities." All of this culminated in 1995 with the Million Man March, televised live on C-Span. While certainly African Americans tuned in, white generation Xers also took note.

The Impact of Black Popular Culture

In addition to the civil rights legacy becoming a staple within mainstream American culture, a fifth contributor to the new reality that made possible hip-hop's crossover explosion was a Black popular culture unique to the 1980s and 1990s. In and of itself, Black popular culture impacting young whites in America wasn't altogether new. But with the new realities of economics and race, Black popular culture became far more influential in the lives of young white Americans.

"With the intense commodification of black popular culture in the post–civil rights era and unprecedented access to it within mainstream commercial culture," writes Mark Anthony

Neale in *Soul Babies: Black Popular Culture and the Post-Soul Aesthetic*, "young blacks were connected to mainstream commercial culture in ways that previous generations had not been. Many black youth who were not living in white suburban spaces could have just as easily been introduced to facsimiles of those environs while watching television shows like *The Brady Bunch, Eight Is Enough*, or *Family Ties*." The same can be said of generation Xers who absorbed urban and suburban Black images from television. For those at the older end of the age-group, shows like *Sandford and Son* (1972–1977), *Good Times* (1974–1979), *The Jeffersons* (1975–1985) and *What's Happening?* (1976–1979) provided that introduction. These early 1970s programs enjoyed strong ratings with Black and white audiences alike, introducing white kids to aspects of the ongoing dialogue Blacks have about race that most whites weren't previously privy to. These shows took on the complexities of race relations in an authentically Black, "laugh to keep from crying" way that would be lost in television programming by the 1980s.

For those generation Xers in the middle of the age-group, *The Cosby Show*, which aired between 1984 and 1992, along with programs like *A Different World* (1987–1993), *Living Single* (1993–1998), *The Martin Lawrence Show* (1992–1997), *In Living Color* (1990–1994), *Family Matters* (1989–1998) and *The Fresh Prince of Bel-Air* (1990–1996), provided similar access. Of course Blacks complain about being portrayed in a negative or stereotypical manner on these programs. But overall, the whole area of post–civil rights era television and Black popular culture is pretty diverse. African Americans are not a

monolith in pop culture—not all representations are stereotypes, and not all are defying them either. Given the increased
importance of popular culture in the lives of American youth
and the increasing visibility of Blacks within it, generation
Xers have come of age with a greater familiarity with some aspects of Black culture than earlier generations.

Music videos further changed the equation by presenting
the "image bite" of Blackness. Now rather than being exclusively confined to the thirty-minute sitcom, Black R&B and
hip-hop videos packaged Blackness into a three-minute snap-
shot. Music videos, primarily through BET and MTV, were
critical cogs in the wheel that moved hip-hop from the mar-
gins to the center of American youth culture. Beginning with
Michael Jackson's music video for "Thriller" in 1983, music
videos became a pivotal tool for selling music and with it a
lifestyle of urban America. Run DMC's "Rock Box" video, the
first rap video to gain heavy rotation on MTV, followed a year
later. That group's rock-rap collaboration with Aerosmith,
"Walk this Way," appeared in 1986, appealing to an emerging
crossover audience. Hip-hop music videos over the years have
covered a gamut of images (from the pathologies of the Black
ghetto to buppie extremism) in a short time period, offering
opportunities for wider Black exposure.

At the same time that music videoes and television were
exposing young whites to varied images of Blackness, Oprah
Winfrey was ascending to American icon status. The *Oprah
Winfrey Show* debuted nationally in 1986. In less than a year,
it was the number one nationally syndicated talk show. In
addition to her business savy and charismatic appeal, the key

to Winfrey's success was her ability to personify American values, speak to stay-at-home-mom and independent feminist sensibilities and maintain her connection to her Black roots, all at the same time. Whether on her own program, or in films like *The Color Purple* or *Beloved*, Oprah presented Americans with an image of Blackness that all could identify with, all the while maintaining Black cultural integrity.

As Oprah was gaining mass appeal among a demographic soon to be known as soccer moms (eclipsing talk show host originator Phil Donahue), another Chicagoan was on the rise. Michael Jordan joined the Chicago Bulls in 1984, averaging 28 points per game his rookie year and leading the NBA in scoring in 1987 (something he would continue through 1992). In 1988 he was named the NBA's Most Valuable Player. Three years later he led the Bulls to the first of what would become a record three consecutive NBA championships, something he'd do again in 1996, 1997 and 1998. How Michael Jordan arrived as one of America's most revered icons must be remembered in context. A predominantly Black NBA was an early 1980s innovation, coming only about ten years before Jordan's first championship. As late as the mid-1970s, the NBA still had a sizable representation of white players. By the 1977–1978 season, the business hadn't yet mastered the science of selling a predominantly Black sport to a mostly white audience—but it would learn to do so almost overnight. In the early 1990s, three NBA championships later, white kids could be found identifying with Jordan as an American hero, right down to sporting the Chicago Bulls number 23 jersey.

All this was par for the course in an America that was beginning to see Blacks in a new light. Many African Americans like Jackson, Oprah, Jordan and Bill Cosby were enjoying the fruits of the civil rights movement. Among other things, civil rights successes were affording Blacks greater visibility and giving whites greater access to Black culture in general. America itself was changing more dramatically than die-hard 1950s nostalgia conservatives and liberals seeking faster, more substantive change were willing to admit.

No analysis of race, popular culture and crossover influence in the 1980s and 1990s is complete without considering the impact of the films of Spike Lee. Earlier films like *She's Gotta Have It* (1986) and *School Daze* (1988) examined the inner workings of Black life: ideas about dating, love and marriage, college life, identity and life aspirations. Films like *Do the Right Thing* (1989), *Jungle Fever* (1991) and *X* (1992) went to the core of American race relations, challenging racism and exploring differences and similarities across the divide. These films were among the most essential definers of the national conversation around race at various moments in the 1980s and 1990s. Cultural critic Nelson George wrote of Spike Lee's films in his *Blackface: Reflections on African Americans and the Movies* (1994):

Critics and op-ed page writers have ground out reams of negative and positive copy about them. Talk shows and college courses have been centered around his efforts. Even everyday conversation has been influenced by his films. For anyone deeply interested in our nation's film culture, he became the first African-American auteur to really matter.

As the 1980s gave way to the 1990s, Black gangsta films like *Boyz N the Hood*, *New Jack City*, *Menace II Society* and *Belly*, often starring well-known hip-hop artists and equipped with hip-hop soundtracks, took over where Spike Lee left off. These films placed a magnifying glass on the new Black youth culture that paralleled the grittier themes of rap music.

The exposure to Black culture that generation Xers enjoyed as a result of mass communications should never be underestimated. Satellite and telecommunications have had one of the most defining influences on Americans this century. In many ways, this exposure has defined the ways we think, live and more. The Black presence in popular culture has changed the way white Americans engage race, especially for a generation of young people who have lived their entire lives with such access.

Other Hip-Hop Specific Factors

What can't be ignored in the rise of hip-hop's popularity among young whites are the concerted pushes and pulls by hip-hop to become mainstream culture. As much as white kids chose hip-hop, hip-hop chose white America. According to pioneers like Kurtis Blow, DJ Kool Herc and Grandmaster Caz, hip-hop always sought to be inclusive, an idea that many say started with Afrika Bambaataa and the Zulu Nation. "Bam was the first major person talking about unity, or people being to-gether," Grandmaster Caz told Joseph Eure and James Spady in their *Nation Conscious Rap* (1991). Caz was speaking about uniting various crews, cliques and gangs, but this concern would later become part of the hip-hop ethos, extending be-yond the Black American community as the Zulu Nation ex-panded internationally. The 1982 hit "Planet Rock" by Afrika Bambaataa and the Soul Sonic Force is still celebrated as a classic among hip-hop kids worldwide.

Inclusiveness was also high on the agenda of those who saw the potential for hip-hop as a business. In their desire for growth, most consciously sought mass appeal. Russell Sim-mons, one of the major forces in helping hip-hop gain promi-nence as an art form and as a culture in mainstream America, writes of his business approach relative to white Americans in his autobiographical *Life and Def: Sex, Drugs, Money and God* (with Nelson George):

> If you are selling Afro Sheen or hair straighteners, your market is defined for you. But what if you're selling a purple suit? Black people may be the chief buyers of purple suits. You may sell most of your purple suits to Black men in the South or Midwest. That doesn't mean, however, that you limit your sales of purple suits to Black people. There may be a whole commu-nity of white buyers who'd love a purple suit, and you should go get that money, too . . . With the interest and heat on urban culture we've seen in the last few years, I'd be crazy not to go for the widest possible audience for what I sell.

Inclusiveness aside, the business of hip-hop offers insight into its appeal to young whites. The business of hip-hop isn't vastly different from any other corporate American industry. While the artistic and creative sides of hip-hop remain largely dominated by Blacks, the business side of the industry is firmly in the hands of white American men, mostly baby boomers. Even Russell Simmons, the business icon of hip-hop, concedes that. Commenting on his experiences in the music world, he writes, "As defined by whites and Blacks, I'd made it. Well that thought turns my stomach, because in comparison to my white counterparts, my company isn't even significant—at least financially."

Wendy Day, who's spent the past thirteen years at the Rap Coalition fighting against record labels' sharecropping system, concurs. "It's very much an industry that is dominated by white men in their fifties," Day says. "That's who is empowered, that's who is running things, that's who can say yea or nay to signing checks. And the music industry is 100 percent run by white corporations. Yes, one is located in Japan; it's still a white corporation. One is located in Germany; it's still a white corporation. One has French and Canadian influence; it's still a white corporation."

On the creative side there are a handful of highly successful Blacks at the top of the midlevel of the chain; for example, P. Diddy, Damon Dash, Master P, but they aren't the ones pulling all the strings. "They [the major labels] found that rather than have employees that understand Black music, it was cheaper to go out and find small labels around the country that were doing the same. The Master Ps, the Cash

Moneys, the Bad Boys, the Rockafellas, the Murder Incorporateds," says Day. "They found it more financially feasible to let somebody else bear the brunt, the risk, the cost of something as simple as employee benefits, a healthcare plan. Why should they have to shoulder that cost when they could just give Puffy a lump check and let him shoulder that for his staff? Whether he goes and buys the Bentley or purchases a healthcare plan for his staff is irrelevant to them. The point is they're saving money off their bottom dollar and that's their goal."

Back on the business side of things, from administration to public relations to marketing right up to the CEO, the hip-hop industry is firmly in the hands of white Americans. In a 2003 interview with Dawn-Elissa Fischer, Education Outreach Coordinator of the Hiphop Archive, Chuck D, when asked about the phrase he coined in 1988 that hip-hop was the Black CNN, put it this way: "I thought it could be used—under the radar—for getting the information out [to] Black communities. It [still] does, but it's not really under the radar. Hip-hop is overstood as a culture. Packaged, endorsed, homogenized. A big white pimp is sitting over it. You can't put soul in a bottle—although they think they've put soul in a bottle." Chuck's comments speak to more than just the white dominance of the hip-hop industry. He's also pointing to the final product. What comes out of the corporate hip-hop industry is packaged and sold as hip-hop, but it is a distortion of hip-hop culture.

With so many whites working in the hip-hop industry, naturally the final product would appeal to other white kids.

Those hip-hop industry insiders, like everyone else, grew up socialized by American culture. That culture informs their thinking from their choice of food or soft drinks to their taste in mu-sic. Most things offensive to mainstream tastes aren't going to saunter past these gatekeepers. Whether it offends Black people—such as the words "niggas," "bitches" and "hos"—is another matter. But if it's offensive to the mainstream you can be sure it won't break through. This isn't necessarily calculated; it's a cultural and financial imperative. The flip side is also true: the white influence is so great in the hip-hop industry that it would be unnatural and odd, almost freakish, if the final product didn't appeal to white youth.

Such dynamics helped hip-hop escape an impending demise, predicted by countless critics in the early 1980s. More than simply a staple in American youth culture, hip-hop has become nearly indistinguishable from it. What was once a marginal culture has become mainstream. When hip-hop was more on the fringe, only a small minority of white kids were engaging it. Most white youth in those early days, like many of their Black, Latino and Asian counterparts, were only remotely aware of its existence. But in the process of becoming synonymous with the mainstream, hip-hop was now another viable option. "To some extent the music is established now," says Jeremy Miller. "It's just become their preference. I've got the option of hearing this great hip-hop, this great rock and roll or something else. For those who choose hip-hop, my guess would be they get that feeling that those of us early on got when they hear it. It's something that moves them like no other music really can. Now that hip-hop is established that's an option that kids can have now that they didn't have before. It may be no different than guys who prefer blonds over brunettes."

———

Today there are hundreds of thousands of young rap artists and mixtape deejays (across race and culture) not only in urban areas, but in small and medium-size cities like Cleveland, Indianapolis, Dallas, Salt Lake City and Albuquerque, pressing their own CDs, selling them on the Internet and "out the trunk." Many routinely perform at the local and regional level. Suburban and rural areas and countless college campuses across the country are rife with local talent as well. These efforts are buttressed by local hip-hop fans eager to celebrate their own homegrown heroes even in the absence of major record deals or national fame. This local level is slowly taking hip-hop back from the corporate industry and is the real future of hip-hop. It's also hip-hop's untold history of the past two decades, where most young people around the nation are tapping into hip-hop's cultural movement.

Complementing this off-the-radar local scene are the many information sources now available about nearly every hip-hop subtopic imaginable: hip-hop artists and their business dealings, how to start a record label, the impact of the Five Percent Nation on hip-hop, the influences of hip-hop on film, bridging the gap between hip-hop and politics and so on. Magazines like *The Source, XXL Vibe, Don Diva* and *Felon* and Web sites like Allhiphop.com, daveyd.com, contrabandit.com, playa-hata.com and countless others cover the gamut. A handful of books by seasoned hip-hop journalists like Joan Morgan *(When Chickenheads Come Home to Roost: My Life as a Hip-Hop Feminist)*, Rob Marriot *(Pimpnosis)*, Smokey Fontaine *(Earl: The Autobiography of DMX)*, Yvonne Bynoe *(Stand and Deliver)*, Scoop Jackson *(Sole Provider)* and Jeff Chang *(Can't Stop, Won't Stop: A History of the Hip-Hop Generation)* have made their way into bookstores and are beginning to provide a theoretical framework and a language for discussing hip-hop, its relationship to mainstream American life and the ways its various subgenres are impacting the culture.

At the high school level educators seek out ways of incorporating hip-hop into the curriculum in order to empower their students. Often they are calling on local hip-hop arts practitioners for their expertise. The same is happening on college campuses, where hip-hop studies is emerging as a discipline. At least seventy-five courses are being offered on hip-hop, according to Stanford University's Hiphop Archive. Another product of this intellectual awakening is the emergence of hip-hop student organizations on college campuses, many of which are multicultural. They are celebrating hip-hop arts, questioning the role of hip-hop as a tool for social change and in many cases assuming the radical role bequeathed by the Black student unions.

With this entire spectrum redefining race in America, by October 2004, Bill O'Reilly's worst nightmare had turned into reality: the ten best-selling artists of *Billboard*'s weekly Top

100 list were Black. A combination of the above five factors collectively created an atmosphere in which it was possible for white kids not only to love hip-hop but embrace it.

Of course, beyond these larger societal influences lie individual choices, circumstances and experiences. The micro influences must also be considered in arriving at any concrete understanding of white kids and hip-hop. These details, as much as the broad strokes, reveal why many young white Americans, like *The Source*'s Jeremy Miller, find in hip-hop a special something that resonates like no other music or cultural moment they've encountered. We now turn in the next chapter to an examination of these micro influences.

2

Identity Crisis?

More Than Acting Black

Let's be honest. All this fascination with hip-hop is just a cultural safari for white people.

—Kevin Powell, *Newsweek* (2003)

In November 1996, *American Demographics* published an article by Marc Spiegler entitled "Marketing Street Culture: Bringing Hip-Hop Styles to the Mainstream," which focused on hip-hop's penetration of white suburban life. Spiegler quoted extensively from Billy Wimsatt's *Bomb the Suburbs*, particularly his views on white kids and hip-hop. In an interview with Wimsatt, Spiegler gleaned further reflections on the types of white kids down with hip-hop, which Spiegler described as "concentric attitudinal rings." Paraphrasing Wimsatt, Spiegler writes:

At the center lie those who actually know Blacks and study the intricacies of hip-hop's culture . . . Next is a group that has peripheral contact with the culture through friends or relatives, but doesn't actively seek "true hip-hopper" status. They go to shows, but don't rap, spray-paint, or breakdance. "After that, you have people who play hip-hop between other types of music," Wimsatt says. "They're sort of free-floating fans." Most white suburban teens probably fall into this category . . . Finally, the people in the outermost circle are . . . rural "wiggers" who avoided cities, and thought Blacks complained too much about their societal lot . . . To Wimsatt, such kids "are pure consumers—they're really into rap, but don't know much, so they're easily manipulated."

The idea of concentric attitudinal circles provides an effective framework for discussing white kids and hip-hop. Of course Wimsatt's analysis is bound to be replete with loopholes, generalizations and oversimplifications—something nearly inescapable when speaking of white kids and hip-hop. Also, Spiegler's piece was published nearly a decade ago, when hip-hop's mass appeal was still emerging. Given the dramatic growth in hip-hop's popularity in the past, these categories, culled from a mid-1990s reality, only hint at the complex space where white kids, hip-hop and race now meet.

Consider Jeremy Miller, the *Source* magazine executive we met in Chapter 1. Jeremy is not the stereotypical white guy who comes to mind when one thinks of white boys into hip-hop. He's 33 years old, a New York University graduate, married and the father of three boys. He doesn't walk the walk or talk the talk of hip-hop; neither does he don the uniform that would announce his affiliation. His six-one, solid country-boy frame and shoulder-length blond locks seem more professional football player in his prime than hip-hop aficionado.

Jeremy was born and raised in a solidly middle-class neighborhood in Warr Acres, Oklahoma, a donut-hole town outside of Oklahoma City. His father graduated from Oklahoma State in the 1960s. Throughout Jeremy's formative years, his stepdad, who adopted him when his mother remarried, vacillated between a wide variety of business ventures and a series of working-class jobs—from construction to hoses and fittings. His mother, who never went to college, worked her way up through the ranks at an airplane title insurance company. She had become the CEO by the time Jeremy entered high school, helping to secure an upper-middle-class lifestyle for the family for the better part of a decade. For Jeremy, this meant family vacations and other comforts, which they enjoyed until his mom was maneuvered out of the company and returned to working low-wage service jobs.

"In a real twist of fate she's now in the same position that my grandma was always in which is almost no money. She vowed she'd never be in that position, but now she's right there."

His family roots are by his account sketchy. "For years we lived under the belief that we had a little bit of Mexican in us mixed in with the typical Oklahoma European mix," Jeremy says of his mother's side of the family. His grandmother was adopted and the family assumed she was half Mexican, but later found out that was false. His father's side of the family also shares what Miller calls the Oklahoma European hodge-podge. "Ask somebody from Oklahoma what they are and they name off about six European countries. A little bit of Danish and German and Irish and French . . . "

Growing up in Warr Acres, Jeremy didn't encounter many people of color. His paternal grandmother had a Black house-keeper whom he adored. He didn't spend a significant amount of time with her, although he recalls her being very nice to him. He also remembers playing with her daughters and hav-ing the time of his life.

The schools he attended were mostly white. There were a handful of Blacks in his high school, maybe 60 out of 1,200 students grades 10–12. His junior high school and elementary school had the same demographics. He only remembers a few Black friends from his childhood.

When he was in sixth grade, he was already six feet tall and everyone thought he would easily hit six-seven. But, as he says, "I only grew an inch taller, and out since then." He dreamed of being a professional football player, but his des-tiny of a career in hip-hop had probably already claimed him. In fact, it was his early pro football dreams that partly led him to hip-hop.

When he was in fifth grade, he attended a four-day summer football camp on a local college campus. Whatever downtime he had away from the field, he spent hanging around the dorm where a bunch of high school guys were listening to music. One of the songs that caught his ear was "Planet Rock," by Afrika Bambaataa and the Soul Sonic Force. When camp ended he rushed home, thumbed through the yellow pages, found the short list of record stores and called every single one until he landed on one who had the record in stock.

"Sound Warehouse was on the south side of Oklahoma City, but it was on my mom's ride home from work. I was a good kid. I didn't get into trouble much and I didn't ask for a whole lot. I called my mom and said, 'Mom can you pick up this record for me on your way home?' She was kinda intrigued by the fact that I was starting to like music. She stopped and got it. To this day 'Planet Rock' is absolutely my favorite song. There's not a song better to me in hip-hop than 'Planet Rock.' It was the first hip-hop record that I ever owned."

"Planet Rock" was actually his second encounter with hip-hop. The first came courtesy of a friend he made in the fourth grade. Mike Bovolini was a white kid who'd moved from New York City to the Oklahoma City area with his parents. Jeremy and Mike hit it off instantly and became best friends. As Jeremy remembers it, they shared a fascination with Black culture—something that soon manifested itself in their musical tastes.

"I would go over to his house to play. One day he said, 'Hold on, I want you to listen to something.' He put Sugarhill Gang's 'Rapper's Delight' on the record player and I can remember sitting there staring at the record player and thinking to myself 'this is amazing, what is this?' I had never heard anything like it in my life."

At the time, Jeremy was absorbed in his father's record collection, which consisted primarily of oldies. "Rapper's Delight," was a natural progression. Mike made a tape of it for

Jeremy using the crude old-school method, a freestanding, big and bulky cassette recorder that picks up all the background sound. But the technicalities didn't matter much. Jeremy played it over and over and over again. Within two weeks he'd memorized all fifteen minutes of "Rapper's Delight."

"That was the day I first heard hip-hop," Jeremy recalls, "and that was the day my life took that turn of having to have anything that sounded like this one song I had heard."

But what he calls his "fascination" with Black people began long before he encountered hip-hop. Jeremy believes this fascination distinguishes white kids into hip-hop. At eight years old, he was already an avid reader who went on his own to the public library to check out books. Black American history already interested him. "I can remember going to the library and looking up 'Afro-American' in the card catalog," he reflects now. Biographies of George Washington Carver, the scientist who discovered more uses for the peanut than you can shake a stick at, and audiotapes of Martin Luther King Jr. that highlighted his great oratorical skill were among his favorites.

"I'm a solid individual thinker, but I remember being affected by movies and TV shows as a kid. I remember being in tears after reading the book *Sounder* and eventually seeing the television movie because I thought it was so unfair what had happened to Black people. Likewise, reading stories about slavery would get me emotional. I understood that it was something really wrong going on in those situations. Maybe it was my early reading on African American history that led me to develop some type of sympathy for the people that were affected by that situation, I don't know."

These encounters are among his first memories of race, but there were others. In junior high school he'd go visit Mike, who'd moved to Houston by that time and lived in a mostly Black apartment complex. This gave him an opportunity to observe the variety in Black American lifestyles. "Some of the best times of my life were going to visit Mike in Houston. There I was able to hang out around more Black kids—not even like the Black kids from my middle-class neighborhood who seemed to be missing something to me. I don't know what it was. Maybe it was more of that rawness of being in a different setting."

His desire to go against the grain pushed him to the Northeast and ultimately to *The Source*. One of his favorite pastimes when he was a college student was keeping a catalog of all the music he owned on a computer database, every twelve-inch, every cassette, every single. "I keep my record collection organized to this day according to the date I bought it, so I can look back and say 'hey what was I doing at this time.' I have my memories based on time periods and the records are still in that order so I can say oh yeah, I remember I bought this record when I was doing such and such. I had this list. I didn't have a clue what I was ever going to do with it except keep myself organized."

He took the catalog, which numbered about 2,000 records, to his interview for an intern position at *The Source*, and it sealed the deal. "After the interview I said, 'By the way, I brought this so you can see that I've got some skills on the computer and that I can keep things organized.' Dave, the publisher, flipped through the list and he gets this weird smirk on his face and says 'Wow I can't believe this.' I know he's think-ing, 'Who is this guy coming in here with this list?' but then he's looking at me kinda like 'this is exactly what we need.'"

This tendency to go against convention and go beyond the ex-pected has long been a part of hip-hop's history, and most certainly is a characteristic of many white kids who love hip-hop. When he graduated from NYU with a degree in market-ing three years later, Jeremy was promoted to an assistant in the circulation department. Over the years, he worked his way up to circulation manager and finally to his current role as chief operating officer.

———

The stereotypes will tell you that all white hip-hop kids speak with a "Black" accent, what journalist Charles Aaron ("What the White Boy Means When He Says Yo," *Spin*, November 1998) calls "b-boy patois," that they fit a certain socioeconomic profile, live in close proximity to Black communities or have been immersed in Black culture. The legions of upper-middle-class and upper-class white kids who love hip-hop defy that stereotype.

At the same time Jeremy was nodding his head to New York City's Afrika Bambaataa and DJ Red Alert, Lynne Ballard* was on the side of the country tuning in to the Bay Area's KDIA. If anyone can exude hippie and high society at the same time,

———

*Some names in this chapter have been changed.

it's Lynne. Articulate and opinionated, but at first glance soft-spoken and shy, she belongs to what has yet to be deemed hip-hop's intellectual elite. Formerly an editor at a national hip-hop magazine, at 30 she now runs a public relations firm that caters to the needs of independent hip-hop acts. From a small, well-lit Beverly Hills office—with her fiercely loyal, mostly white-haired cat Slim Shady (named after the world's most famous white rapper) at her side—she goes above and beyond the call of duty for underground hip-hop artists scratching to make their way in a hip-hop environment too often dictated by the corporate-dominated hip-hop industry.

"It's almost like social activism in a way because I can work with people who are really artists, political artists and artists outside the box who would never get play by majors," she says. "The independent hip-hop scene is full of artists that don't fit into the major label structure. I have no interest in trying to promote that commercial, garbage, pop message."

Identifying a void is one of the things that became second nature for many generation Xers in their late twenties and early thirties who, like Lynne, found themselves working in the hip-hop industry as it made the leap to the mainstream. She's one of the white hip-hop heads who got down with hip-hop long before its mainstream acceptance. "In the '80s it was way more a political thing to do because it was non-mainstream," she says, thinking back to the days when she fell in love with hip-hop. "You were really going against the grain to do it." She echoes Jeremy's belief that for white kids, both then and now, there is on some level a fascination with Black culture. "But to-day when I think of all these white girls and boys who wear cornrows and appropriate hip-hop culture, most of them are unaware of the struggle. In the '80s to be a white person into hip-hop, you were making a political statement."

Describing Lynne as a 1970s-style hippie would be simplifying the matter. Though she's a graduate of the University of California–Berkeley, she's not the child of radicals you might suspect. "My dad is a Bush supporter. He's very right-wing and at the same time, he's a little out of touch with American culture. He was so impressed I got into Berkeley, [but] he didn't know what they were known for. He just knew it was a good school. It's not like he thought, I'm going to send her here and she's going to get all political."

Her mother came from an upper-middle-class family, about ten generations of Americans, that had been in California for four—a combination of British, Italian, Irish and French descent. In the 1950s, her father, who is of Russian descent, immigrated to the United States from Japan, where he was born into a family of Russian immigrants (although he never lived in Russia). "Culturally, he's 100 percent Japanese," Lynne says. After arriving in the United States with $200, he found his way to San Francisco and created a successful business importing and exporting.

Lynne grew up in San Francisco's Pacific Heights area, where she attended a Catholic elementary school and a private junior high. In the late 1980s she enrolled at the Branson School, one of the most elite private high schools in the country. "We used to call Branson 'the country club.' If your parents didn't buy you a brand-new car for your sixteenth birthday, you were the horror of the school," she recalls. "And if you crashed it, then your dad got you a new one."

Located in Ross, California, where the average home costs $1 million, Branson wasn't exactly a model of diversity. Out of a class size of around one hundred at Branson, Lynn recalls only one Black student per class. Her Catholic elementary school was a bit more diverse, with Black students making up around 25 percent of the student body. But at her junior high the ratio was nearly as lopsided as at Branson. During those formative years, she always, to her father's chagrin, sought out the Black students as friends. The pattern continued during junior high and at the Branson School, even though there were few Black students.

"My dad always made me feel bad that I had Black friends. The very first day [of junior high], I end up hanging out and talking with the one Black girl in my class. My brother saw me do that and he was like 'Dude, what are you doing? You've gotta make another friend.' So it was always something that I knew my dad didn't totally approve of."

For Lynne, there was no defining hip-hop moment. She started collecting music, including but not limited to hip-hop, at age 13. In college she bought her first mixer and began dabbling in deejaying. Although she doesn't recall a specific rap song that stands out in her mind, Grandmaster Flash and Sugarhill Gang are part of her extensive vinyl collection. Her introduction to hip-hop was more personal than Jeremy's. Her relationship with her nanny, Donna, defined her early interest in the music and the culture.

Some of Lynne's earliest memories of hip-hop are of listening along to the radio with her nanny. "That's all I knew. I just remember from a really early age being really into it. I just liked it and I never really knew anything else because that's what Donna always had on the radio."

Her relationship with Donna went far beyond child care. Lynne's mother died of cancer when Lynne was eight. She knew she was dying and asked Donna to stay on to provide the children with a sense of consistency. Strangely enough, Donna's own mother was murdered during a robbery at that time. She went back to West Virginia to bury her mother, for what she thought would be a week. While she was gone, Lynne's mother died. When Donna returned, she continued to live with the family until Lynne and her brother went off to college. Donna was a major presence in Lynne's formative years. Now well into her eighties, she remains a significant part of Lynne's life.

"In a lot of ways Donna served as a buffer. She was soft and she understood what we were going through dealing with my dad. Here we were this wealthy family and we had to put on a pretense that even though my mom died, we were going to be okay. Meanwhile we were crumbling inside." Lynne explains that her father's uncontrollable bouts of rage (extreme verbal abuse) were directed at Donna as often as they were at his children.

"Donna saw the truth. She was our safety net. She would listen to us vent for hours and she would understand. I remember thinking here we are with all this money and we're totally screwed up, and here is this Black woman who had all the sympathy in the world for us.

"My early love for hip-hop was in part a revolt to growing up in a very upper-class, extremely closed society where I saw firsthand that money doesn't bring happiness. I was so disgusted with the society I lived in. But then there's this parallel life where I've always had Black friends, and I have always had Donna."

W.E.B. Du Bois describes the Black American experience as demanding "double-consciousness," a passion filled with equal parts love and loathing. Hearing Lynne speak of her father conjures up that feeling. She speaks with great fondness of the international perspective her father ingrained in her as a child, including extensive travel on family trips to countries like Turkey, Israel, Haiti and Egypt.

Over the years, she's even grown accustomed to her father's conservative politics—though diametrically opposed to her own. But his racial politics makes her skin crawl. "True to his Japanese upbringing, he hates Koreans. He also shares the idea that because Black people are the darkest, then they're the lowest on the totem pole—although he would never admit to this."

She recalls her father's "concern" when she befriended a group of Black girls in elementary school.

"What's your problem? Why do you only have Black friends?"

"I don't know why. What's wrong with it anyway?"

"They just do things differently than us."

"Like what?"

"They eat different foods."

"That next day I asked my best friend, Paula, 'What did you have for dinner last night?' And it was something basic like steak and potatoes."

It was a combination of Donna's presence and her father's running commentary that made Lynne think more deeply about race. "I've always felt Blacks got a raw deal," she says, trying to think back to when she first became aware of race. She points to an occasion when she was four or five years old and watching the TV drama *Adam 12*. She turned to her father and asked, "Why are all the bad people on TV Black?"

"Because that's the way it is!" he shot back. It was a recurring response that, like another of his favorite one-liners, Lynne came to think of as "just my dad's racist views."

"The educated ones are different," he'd say to explain away his prejudice toward Black Americans. "When I meet an educated Black person, I see no color." Lynne in part attributes this to her father's being a product of his time but also to his immigrant experiences, which dictated a racial caste system rooted in international geopolitics. "He's racist in a really interesting way, not like a redneck way, but in a way where he identifies everybody by their race, like 'that Greek guy,' 'that such and such guy,'" she says, as if trying to make sense of it to herself. "For him race has everything to do with everything. That's how he qualifies everyone. He grew up white in a xenophobic society and he's highly aware of race. He's probably given that to me. Because he's been so racist, I've probably developed some sort of backlash to that."

At Berkeley, Lynne majored in ethnic studies. It was in an introduction to Black studies course that she first felt comfortable with academics. That semester her grades skyrocketed. Prior to that, she says, she was always a good student but she was never really into school. At times she felt like an outcast. "Everybody there was into the Grateful Dead," she says of her classmates at Branson. "But I was sneaking out to Run DMC concerts. I was always shunned for going against the grain. You know, people were like 'Oh God, there's Lynne.'"

Some of the schoolmates who used to laugh behind her back now have a better appreciation for her view of the world. These are the types of white kids appropriating hip-hop she finds annoying. Those who were into hip-hop back in 1980s, in the pre-mainstream era, were down for the struggle to create new racial politics. By contrast, kids now are not as political. "To me it breaks down along age lines. Many of the younger kids don't even get it. This is just the way they've grown up. They've seen Nelly on TV or Ja Rule or whatever and this is the way society is today. They don't put it into context."

This may be a bit of ageism; older hip-hop kids looking down on the newjacks in a we-walked-five-miles-to-school-in-the-snow kind of way. But without a doubt the range of hip-hop's influence has widened among white youth, who are absorbing its perceptions and effects into their worldviews.

Lynne's criticism of whites and hip-hop spills over into her assessment of the music industry and its racism. "There is racism in the hip-hop industry for sure. You can see it in the fact that Eminem's been able to sell so many more albums and in the way that he'll get played on K-ROQ *and* on urban stations. Meanwhile Kanye doesn't get played on both. Eminem is able to appeal to a larger demographic because he's white. And there is absolutely racism in that many of the label owners and radio stations are owned by white people and the images of Blacks that they are choosing to put out there are a parody. MTV has really gotten behind these artists who represent the one small fraction that degrades and humiliates Black culture. It's not even about the music or the culture any more; it's just all about money."

Despite her criticism of hip-hop, it's been a central, defining element of Lynne's life. "If you look at what has happened to Black people in this country you can basically learn all you need to know about the government and the way it's set up, and the inequities. It's a large part of how I see the world. Because hip-hop is a culture of resistance, it's given me the ability to think critically and I take that with me to everything I do, from my career choice over the past eight years of my life to how I look at any president's administration to how I look at any political issue. Always a part of that thought process is how anything is affecting the hip-hop generation and more specifically how it's affecting African Americans."

———————

Lynne's outlook brings us back to the concentric attitudinal circles of white kids down with hip-hop. Naming four categories, as Lynne's and Jeremy's experiences reveal, may be overstating the range, partly because those categories overlap given today's hip-hop reality. Wimsatt's first category, "those who actually know Blacks and study the intricacies of hip-hop culture," is no longer limited to hip-hop arts practitioners alone. Wimsatt's second category, nonpractioners who have "peripheral contact with hip-hop culture through friends or relatives," is problematic in that almost all young Americans by now fit this description. In today's context, it's a nonexistent or irrelevant category. His third and fourth categories overlap as well, as there isn't much difference between "free-floating fans who listen to accessible hip-hop groups" and "pure consumers." In fact, pure consumers can be found in all of these categories. And all whites who have been immersed in American racism carry racist baggage and believe, for example, "Blacks complain too much" (Wimsatt's fourth category). And all know more about hip-hop than the average white kid (or Black kid for that matter) living in the early 1980s, when hip-hop was still off the radar and still, for the most part, an underground culture. Now hip-hop is not only mainstream—with its own magazines, television programs, film, videos in regular rotation on MTV and BET and prominent appearances from the Grammy Awards to the Super Bowl halftime show. It's become woven into the fabric of American popular culture.

It may help us to better understand the concentric circles of white hip-hop kids if we imagine corresponding Black circles. Consider Black kids who love hip-hop in *three* concentric attitudinal rings. The smallest circle would contain those Blacks most detached from Black youth culture: those tuning in to hip-hop simply as another pop cultural form, the occasional hip-hop listener. The stereotypical "buppie" type who, operating out of sense of elitism, feels advocates of street culture are lost souls. In the second, slightly larger circle are those along for the pop culture ride: those immersed in American consumer culture who consume hip-hop along with other must-have commodities. Third would be practitioners of the arts of hip-hop culture, along with those for whom the culture is life and death. Here you'd also find kids who know and love Black youth culture because it is their life. To some extent they too live hip-hop, as a Black youth subculture. Of course, the boundaries of these three categories overlap. If ordered by size, the second and third categories could be exchanged.

A more accurate "concentric attitudinal rings" framework for white kids and hip-hop would include three rings. The first, at the center, concurs with Wimsatt's analysis: actual practitioners of the arts of hip-hop culture. The first, however, is interchangeable with the second ring moving outward: white kids deeply immersed in Black youth culture and Black American culture, who understand and appreciate hip-hop as contemporary Black youth culture. These white Americans, whether or not they are hip-hop arts practicioners themselves, are at ease with Blacks, don't consider Blacks a novelty and recognize race as a false construct. (Still, these folks carry racist baggage—as we all do, African Americans included, courtesy of our old racial politics upbringing.)

Finally, the third and largest ring contains free-floating fans: general music fans of today's pop culture with no hard-core allegiance to any one genre. They are attached to hip-hop through the hip-hop artists they love for the moment as the dominant pop music, though no more deeply than they love Britney Spears or Justin Timberlake. Kids in this category love hip-hop because it's the dominant youth culture.

Jeremy and Lynne (both in their early thirties) fall into the middle of the hip-hop generation age-group. Those in their younger teens to early twenties, technically the millennium generation, have a similar but still unique take on hip-hop.

They came of age with hip-hop mostly as an established phenomenon, rather than an emerging one. The civil rights movement and Jim Crow laws are even more ancient history to them than to their hip-hop generation older siblings. For these kids, hip-hop has been mainstream culture for nearly all their lives.

Janice Fisco, 19, falls into this age-group. When she was still in elementary school, her father took her to the Meadowlands, where he'd arranged for her to meet living legend Michael Jordan after an NBA game. It was the New Jersey Nets against Chicago as the Bulls were settling into a season that would end in a three-peat championship. She was nine years old.

"There was a big crowd of people and he [Jordan] picked me up high in the air. I remember he told me if I didn't smile for the picture, he'd drop me. And I smiled and they took the picture."

In addition to allowing her to meet basketball greats, her father's work in the professional basketball industry provided her greater access to Blacks in pop culture than the average American kid, white or Black. The NBA, second only to hip-hop, has been a primary source of cross-racial interaction, above and beyond baseball (even given Jackie Robinson's historic color-barrier breaking), and including the military. Beyond merely observing and feeling the influence of professional athletes on American popular culture, Janice met the celebrity athletes themselves. While most American families may have casual dinner discussions about celebrity entertainers, the conversations she was privy to at home were coupled with interaction with actual sports stars, from telephone calls to visits in her home.

"Growing up I never really thought race was an issue," says Janice, who lived on Manhattan's Lower East Side. At the start of her junior year in high school, her family moved out to Long Island, after years of spending summers in the Hamptons. "I knew that Blacks definitely dominated the NBA. And even when I met Michael Jordan, I thought of him as this huge superstar but it was never like I thought of him as a 'Black' athlete. There was never that distinction. My parents never really talked about race, either negatively or positively. I grew up never really seeing any difference between a Black person and a white person."

Not that she'd never heard members of her extended family spout racist views. It was her dating choices that sparked this in her grandmother, inspiring her to more openly share views that otherwise were never up for discussion. Early in high school, she started dating a boy named John. He was Black, very fair skinned, tall and handsome. Janice's grandmother didn't vehemently protest this.

"But she could never accept me dating Martin. He's really dark and he's got those very Black features. And my grandmother would talk about his wide nose all the time."

Janice, now a senior in college, is trying to develop a radar for closet racists. She thinks they are the most serious threats to American race relations: individuals who harbor racist views that only make guest appearances, albeit strong ones.

"You start to realize that there are really people out there like that and what's even more amazing is that there's so many people you don't even know who are racist."

Her dating choices and her grandmother's response to them helped her realize that race was something that would always be part of her life. She wonders if her parents deemphasizing race was a bad thing.

"My parents never made race a big deal. It was never how they identified someone. I think that is a good thing, but it's also a bad thing because it made me a little too naive. Once I did realize it meant something and once I realized it was going to mean something in my life because of the company I was keeping, it shattered me for a while. I realized race was going to end up causing a problem for me even if not in my family or among my own friends then in the public in some way."

For those coming of age in America, even in the post–civil rights age, racism has an uncanny way of making its presence felt. Janice's earliest memories of race involve her first high school boyfriend, Naim, an Egyptian immigrant she dated when she was in the tenth grade.

"I knew he was Muslim. And I knew his family was pretty strict with it. He was two years older than me and told me right up front that his parents could never know about me."

On their first date, they went to a coffee shop in Manhattan. "We were sitting in the back and these two high society–type white women were staring at us the entire time. They stared us down to the point where I felt uncomfortable. But even that kind of eluded me a little bit."

A more striking incident came a little later. One day they were walking down the street together during a parade. "Out of nowhere Naim said, 'I hate those Jews,' or something like that. I loved this guy and still love him to this day. I think he's a great guy, but he had that side to him."

Even though she grew up in the so-called melting pot, Janice's day-to-day existence was most segregated. She recalls no Black families living in her neighborhood that she knew. "I didn't really come across that many Black families in school until I moved to Long Island."

Janice finished up high school at a private school in the area. The school she attended, with an enrollment of fewer than three hundred students in grades 5–12, draws students from a variety of small villages on the eastern end of Long Island. One of the Hamptons' best-kept secrets is the handful of vibrant Black communities tucked across the tracks from village commercial districts and multimillion-dollar mansions and ignored by elites: the working-class Black communities of Bridgehampton, Southampton and Easthampton. Janice's class size was about forty students. Aside from one Black guy, an Asian girl, and a Native American girl, all of her classmates were white. Still, just by being on the far east end of Long Island and attending such a small school, there was a lot of interaction between private school students and those who attended the nearby public schools, as area schools collaborated to make up teams to compete with schools with larger student pools.

Janice's elementary and high school experiences in New York City, despite *Brown v. Board of Education* almost a quarter of a century earlier, were segregated by both race and class. She attended a prestigious private girls school for most of high school. Her grade included about sixty students who were divided among three classes; three of the sixty girls were Black. A handful of students were from impoverished and socially neglected neighborhoods. The rest came from a variety of elite backgrounds, literally billionaire daughters. Among Janice's classmates were the children of ambassadors, CEOs of Fortune 500 corporations and well-known elected officials. As she moved into her high school years, she began to feel that the school was too "snobby" and not really her preference.

"We lived downtown in Peter Cooper. We didn't have a doorman, but it wasn't like there were drug dealers on every corner. Our school was uptown. The girl who had been my best friend since seventh grade, her father was the U.S. ambassador to a country in South America. Either her mother wouldn't let her or she decided, like other kids in our school, that she wouldn't come downtown. Most of the kids I went to school with were really rich kids who lived on Park Avenue not far from our school. By the tenth grade I was feeling like I just didn't fit in."

That her boyfriend, Naim, went to public school downtown didn't help matters. Since she had no friends left at school, she began spending part of her school day afternoons alone in the dark room developing film. She associates one of her first memories of hip-hop with these afternoons of solitude. "In the darkroom, we were allowed to listen to the radio. I vividly remember Biggie's song 'Hypnotize.' We listened to Hot 97 all the time when I was growing up, but I really never got into hip-hop until that song came on. It was then that I started buying CDs." This was the height of hip-hop's arrival in the mainstream. The "East Coast–West Coast war" was in full swing.

Janice also has faint memories of her mother playing hip-hop on the radio when she was younger. "One of the reasons I love hip-hop is because of the rhythm. Unless it's like a really good rapper, I don't think I'm buying it for the words. My mom always loved rap and she loved to dance when I was growing up. I remember we would always turn the radio dial to Hot 97 and dance together. My mom worked at a Catholic school in Williamsburg, Brooklyn, as a teacher before I was born. There were a lot of Blacks and Hispanics in the school. She would tell me and my brother stories about back in the day when she would go around the corner from the school and witness b-boy battles right on the street."

It's been a decade since the day Janice, cradled high in the sky in Michael Jordan's big hands, nervously smiled for the camera. Now she speculates about how the pop culture landscape of her formative years compares to today's dominant pop culture influences, which have shifted from Michael Jordan to 50 Cent. She remembers more recently venturing into the Black side of her college town to buy 50 Cent's debut album *Get Rich or Die Tryin'* the day it went on sale in February 2003. Other than The Clipse CD *Lord Willin'*, which she bought on a whim, she hadn't bought a CD in a while. The street buzz on 50 Cent piqued her curiosity.

"Best Buy was selling it for $9.99. Millennium Music, which is right next to the campus, was selling it for $18.99 or something crazy like that. I didn't mind taking a little drive." Best

Buy is about a half hour drive from the campus. It was a bright, sunny winter day. The store opened at 10:00 A.M., and Janice stood in line for fifteen minutes. She notes she was the only female and the only white person on the line.

Despite her observation, her race radar isn't one-dimensional. This is apparent when I ask her about hip-hop and white kids. She says she thinks white girls into hip-hop have gotten a bad rap. It's something she's very sensitive about. "I remember Mace had that one skit on his CD *Harlem World* where he calls up these two white girls. I never took offense to it because it really sounded like a stupid white girl who's impressed with this Black rapper calling her up."

And while she considers herself a feminist, she isn't offended by the extensive use of the b-word, whose usage in hip-hop she finds to be pretty generalized rather than directed specifically to Black women. She says she always thought of the word "bitch" as representing strength.

"I had this trainer I rode with from the time I was six years old until I was twelve," she says. "She ran a farm out in the Hamptons and if she got into a fight with you and threw you off her farm, you weren't allowed back in the driveway. People called her a bitch all the time, but I loved her because she was very, very strong. So from the time I was a kid, I thought that was a strong word."

What also bothers her is the assumption that white kids are hip-hop's dominant audience, which suggests that Black kids more and more are seen as a nonfactor even in hip-hop. "If Black kids aren't listening to hip-hop, then what are they listening to?" she reasons. It's a question that won't go away.

Along with Janice, Lynne and Jeremy, there are countless other young whites, from elementary school age to those well into their thirties, who don't fit any easy categorization. What about those working in the hip-hop industry, peripheral to the arts, whose day-to-day work influences the commercial side of hip-hop culture? What about those deep into the hip-hop underground?

Why do white kids love hip-hop? The answers are endless. But the further you dig into individual lives, the more layers of complexity you're likely to find. Race in America is complicated by many factors. Old racial politics and new racial politics collide with regional differences, personal experience, family history, pop culture and individual experience. Each person has a unique story that brought him or her to hip-hop. Looking at the micro-reasons as well as the macro ones help us make sense of a contemporary hip-hop scene in which a new generation is affected by America's racial history and in the process is constructing a new politics.

Hip-hop is not a panacea. It is not a cure-all that will bring the races together in a "We Are the World" fashion. As Elliot Wilson, editor in chief of the hip-hop magazine *XXL,* told the *New York Times* in its How Race Is Lived in America series, "Who because of hip-hop now believes, I've seen the light. I'm going to save the Blacks?"

Instead, hip-hop is a framework, a culture that has brought young people together and provides a public space that they can communicate within unrestricted by the old obstacles. Simultaneously, young whites are engaging with Black youth culture just as corporate culture has become a tool for marketing everything, even Blackness, via pop culture. In short, America has changed. Todd Boyd, author of *The New HNIC: The Death of Civil Rights and the Reign of Hip-Hop*, gave a lecture at the University of San Diego, February 17, 2004. He said, "With the racial barriers down, [referring to the end of legal segregation] people can now gravitate toward what they like." But does such a cultural buffet, by definition, mean that young whites are the primary audience?

3

Erasing Blackness

Are White Suburban Kids
Really Hip-Hop's Primary Audience?

Rich kids go and cop the *Source*
They don't know about the blocks I'm on.
—Nas, *Got Yourself a Gun*

I n November 1991 an article written by David Samuels, entitled "The Rap on Rap: The Black Music That Isn't Either,"
appeared in the *New Republic.* The premise of the piece was
what the subtitle suggested: that Blacks were neither the force
behind the business of hip-hop nor hip-hop's primary consumer audience. Sidestepping hip-hop's pioneers, Samuels
strategically pointed to the influence of Rick Rubin, who is
white and founded Def Jam Records in 1983 before later making Russell Simmons his partner.* He highlights that it was the

---

*Although he makes a passing reference late in the piece to DJ Kool
Herc and his Jamaican roots as well as Sylvia Robinson, he ignores the

Beastie Boys, a white punk band turned rap group, that was the first hip-hop group to have an album go platinum *(Licensed to Ill)* in 1988. Samuels also notes the rising influence of the hip-hop magazine *The Source* and emphasized that its founder and editor in chief, John Schecter, was an upper-middle-class white Harvard graduate.** As if that wasn't white enough, according to Samuels, hip-hop's audience "is primarily composed of white suburban males."

Samuels never specified a percentage; he just claimed that "although rap is still proportionately more popular among blacks, its primary audience is white and lives in the suburbs." However, by February 2004, over a decade later, *Forbes* magazine ("The Business of Hip-Hop: A Billion-dollar Industry," February 18, 2004) reported that of an estimated 45 million hip-hop consumers between 13 and 34, 80 percent were white. From the moment Samuels's story appeared in 1991 right up to the present, countless news publications, books, hip-hop industry insiders and commentators have made similar references to the number of white hip-hop fans, varying from 60 to 80 percent of the buying audience. Few cite a source for this statistic.

---

groundwork laid by Blacks throughout the diaspora—not just African Americans, such as Afrika Bambaataa, Lovebug Starsky and others—in bringing hip-hop into existence. The implication is that white Americans made hip-hop happen as a business, both on the production and on the consuming end, which isn't an accurate history.

**At the time Samuels wrote, however, *The Source* had three additional owners: David Mays, who is white, James Bernard and Ed Young, both of whom are Black, a point Samuels conveniently fails to mention.

The rarely disputed "fact" that white suburban youth con-stitute hip-hop's primary audience may now be as popular as hip-hop itself. But search high and low and you would be hard-pressed to find a source for it. Even harder to find would be a demographic study that substantiates it. More likely, such a search would reveal a nationwide game of Telephone, where one whispered thought gets twisted and exaggerated beyond recognition. How has a statistic with so little hard data to back it up become so widely referenced and accepted?

At the center of this myth making sits a market research company founded to track music sales. In 1991 Michael Shalett and Michael Fine came up with a method of tracking over-the-counter sales for the music industry. Shalett and Fine named their brainchild Soundscan. Prior to Soundscan, the music industry—including the *Billboard* charts—had to rely on rec-ord stores to periodically report their fifty top-selling albums. This approach took months. By contrast, Soundscan, using a computerized scanning system, could put sales figures at the fingertips of record labels in a week. Coming out of the gate in 1991, Soundscan was tracking approximately 7,300 retail out-lets, mostly chain stores in the suburbs. Before Soundscan, the majority of stores that reported sales were freestanding stores in urban areas. This discrepancy was one of the earliest criti-cisms of Soundscan—its data pool was lopsided to begin with, hence the seeming overnight shift of hip-hop's audience from the hood to the suburbs.

By now the chief observers of music industry sales have, for the most part, evaded the early criticism. Today the company proudly claims to track around 19,000 stores and growing. In recent years, it has even begun tracking music sales down-loaded from Internet sites like iTunes.

Soundscan's knack for staying two steps ahead of the game gave it an edge over would-be competitors. As early as 1991, the company realized that it was only scratching the surface in its attempts to understand music consumers. Because Sound-scan only tallies quantities of over-the-counter sales, within a year, the company established a subsidiary venture, Soundata, to conduct surveys of active music consumers for a more ac-curate picture of consumer demographics and buying habits. In 1992 Soundata conducted monthly surveys of roughly 2,000 active music consumers, people who bought from fif-teen to twenty CDs a month.* On the subject of white kids and hip-hop, the survey only asked these consumers if they bought "hard-core hip-hop" in the past six months, nothing more.** Eight percent of whites, accounting for 64 percent of sales, said they had. Soundata didn't do another survey until 1995, when it asked consumers, "How do you feel about rap music?" Twenty-four percent of whites said they liked rap. But again the Soundata surveys didn't continue annually. The next sur-vey, entitled "The Soundata National Consumer Study," wasn't

---

*This is based on my interview with Shalett in 1994.
**Hard-core hip-hop in the mid- to late 1980s was defined as true hip-hop as opposed to the watered-down commercial stuff that was emerg-ing with greater frequency as independent labels buckled under the consolidation of the music industry. With the rise of so-called gangsta rap by the late 1980s and early 1990s, mainstream media outlets began equating "hard-core" with so-called gangsta.

conducted until 1998. This time the survey shied away from asking any questions about white kids and hip-hop.

It was the launching of Soundscan in the summer of 1991 (not Soundata's demographic surveys, the first of which wouldn't come until a year later) that served as the basis for David Samuels's *New Republic* revelations later that fall. Yet Soundscan's debut wasn't the origin of the idea that white kids were hip-hop's primary consumers. Record label executives themselves were already balking at the idea that Black teens could account for the significant sales hip-hop had begun posting in the late 1980s. In 1991, artists like NWA *(EFIL4ZAGGIN)*, Ice Cube *(America's Most Wanted)* and Naughty By Nature *(Naughty By Nature)* were already selling upward of a million units each. Prior to this, hip-hop had been mostly a gold sales affair; to be considered a major rap star, an artist only needed to reach 500,000 units in sales. By the early 1990s, though, those numbers were quickly proving insignificant for a rap artist seeking to establish himself or herself as a significant player. The early results of Soundscan's computerized system seemingly gave substance to existing assumptions.

"There are more young whites in the U.S. than Blacks," Mike Shalett said in an interview with me in 1994, when I asked him about hip-hop's white listening audience. "And Soundata's monthly survey suggests overwhelming sales to white teens. Hence, it's a fair assumption to say white teens are rap's greatest buying audience." According the 1990 census, there were roughly 35 million white teens in the United States as compared to 7 million Black teens.

In the mid-1990s, hip-hop further penetrated American pop culture. With platinum sales now the standard for success in the growing hip-hop industry, the idea that hip-hop's primary audience was white and suburban overshadowed hip-hop's rise. Whenever hip-hop met resistance on its mainstream ascension through concert venues, corporate advertising, department stores, Hollywood and most recently Broadway, this notion of a primarily white audience lessened the blow for those steeped in America's old racial politics. In 1963 Malcolm X discussed the "Black revolution" and the "Negro revolution" with a poignant analogy to coffee: "What do you do when you have coffee that's too Black? You weaken it with cream." The idea of a white primary audience became hip-hop's cream, ready, willing and able to dilute what was considered by many Americans far too Black and far too influential.

In 1997 Soundscan was bought by Nielsen, of television ratings fame, and was renamed Nielsen-Soundscan. Of course the company still encounters the occasional critic who challenges the claim that its sales numbers can't be manipulated. (In July 2001 a *Los Angeles Times* article reported that in fact record labels could and had found a way to inflate their sales.) But Nielsen-Soundscan is so firmly positioned in the music industry that not even this could poke a hole in its armor. In Nielsen-Soundscan, record labels and retailers believe they've found the holy grail.* Now re-

---

*One local independent record chain in the Boston area claimed that Soundscan used its sales against it and consequently stopped reporting sales, despite the benefits that doing so afforded them with record labels. (Thea Singer, "Are You Giving Away Too Much Information About Your Business?" *Inc.* March 16, 1999, p.38.)

tailers can buy more strategically. Now record labels can more specifically say where many of their CDs are selling throughout the country—information unavailable in the pre-Soundscan world. But some took Soundscan's data too far. In 1992 Dr. Dre's *The Chronic* (featuring Snoop Dogg) sold 3 million units, according to Interscope, using Soundscan data. Based on the strength of these sales and data reports, the myth that gangsta rap was mostly selling in the suburbs was born.

Like record executives before them, record label operatives in the mid-1990s made similar pronouncements when media outlets periodically came a-calling—all too eager to sound off on the Black music that allegedly more white kids consume than Blacks. The assumption was fast becoming hard truth.

None of this was directly endorsed by Nielsen-Soundscan, although the company is often identified as the source. In Nielsen-Soundscan's defense, although the company prides itself on being able to obtain demographic data and conduct-controlled searches of hip-hop sales in a given area, none of the searches or data they compile specify race, nor do they target suburban versus rural neighborhoods. Rather, Sound-scan breaks data down into categories such as "high-income" and "low-income" areas, not in terms of Black and white, suburban or urban. So those record labels concluding that "high-income" means suburban and white, and "low-income" means urban and Black are doing so based on sub-jective analysis—equating income areas with race, not on hard data gathered by Soundscan. A Soundscan spokesperson concurs: "A variety of conclusions can be drawn depending on how they are looking at the data, but any conclusions reached about white kids and black kids, suburban and urban involves a fair amount of conjecture." But these aren't the only loopholes in the argument that white kids are hip-hop's primary audience. Consider the following:

1. The nebulous 10 percent off the Soundscan radar.   Nielsen-Soundscan claims that it currently tracks 90 percent of the market, a remarkable percentage for any industry.* In determining sales, it estimates the remaining 10 percent of sales that aren't tracked. But just as the company does not record consumers' race, the company can't make an actual racial breakdown on sales it isn't actually tracking—neither does it attempt to do so. Mom-and-pop stores, local corner stores and bodegas that sell CDs, booths at flea markets, small independent record stores operating on shoestring budgets, and the like, which don't report their sales to Nielsen-Soundscan, all fall into this 10 percent category. Add to that big retailers such as Starbucks, Hallmark, Burlington Coat Factory and others who opt out of Soundscan in the interest of keeping their store information private.

Nielsen-Soundscan requires stores to have the capacity to report sales electronically. Stores reporting to Nielsen-Soundscan must also regularly carry a minimum of twelve titles. If the bulk of that remaining 10 percent of the market includes substantial hip-hop sales to consumers who aren't white, then the record labels' percentages would shift a bit. If the figure is closer

---

*By contrast, the influential *New York Times* Bestsellers list is only representing about 4,000 stores in an industry that claims over 50,000 retailers.

to, say, 50–60 percent, that 10 percent could mean the difference in hip-hop's consumer audience being either half or less than half white. This would also make a big difference in the apparent influence of those currently considered hip-hop's "primary audience."

Even with formulas to account for the 10 percent, according to the *New York Times*, "counting CD sales is not an exact science": "While no one knows how many sales go unreported, a conservative estimate is in the millions . . . some albums, especially budget discs, various ethnic music albums and a variety of compilations—never make it into the final total" ("Counting CD Sales Is Not an Exact Science," November 24, 2003, p. C8). And bear in mind that sales numbers reflect purchases of new, not used, CDs, which means a lot in today's music-consuming climate where albums are routinely lackluster. Furthermore, today's picky consumers, given music and computer technology, have options, from buying bootleg CDs to purchasing mixtapes to downloading songs from the Internet.

2. Untracked and untrackable music downloading. The countless individuals downloading hip-hop songs from the Internet, some for a fee and many for free, are too substantial to ignore. This is another unquantifiable number of consumers whose racial identity is impossible to determine. For years the industry ignored downloaded music—except of course when kicking and screaming about how it was being crippled by the Internet. Until July 2003, Nielsen-Soundscan didn't track any downloaded music at all. The belated attempt to track this method for accessing music is odd, given that CD sales from

2000 to 2002 decreased by 100 million units (from 785 million units to 681 million units), according to Nielsen-Soundscan. In 2002 Nielsen-Soundscan began tracking download companies who charge a fee for downloaded music, like Musicmatch and iTunes. It found that more than 19.2 million digital tracks were sold online in the last six months of 2003. Still unaccounted for are the vast quantities of music downloaded for free. It is impossible to track these numbers, and it is equally impossible to make determinations about race regarding downloaded music. As methods for tracking downloaded music evolve, if the past is any indication, assumptions about race will emerge. Most likely they will be centered around the overhyped idea of the digital divide—that Black Americans are disproportionately locked out of the information superhighway; naturally this would include music downloading.* Even in an age of an emerging new racial politics, such easy conclusions will die hard.

Industry sympathizers attribute the most recent drop in sales growth to Internet downloading, but fans cite other variables, most notably lackluster albums rife with mediocre offerings. Three to five songs worth listening to per album has become the norm. Plenty of young people, regardless of race, have turned to Internet downloading out of convenience, necessity or just common sense—despite threats of lawsuits from the music industry. Many high school and college students around the country say that this is the only way they obtain music. But other options exist beyond downloading,

---

*In 2003, 43 percent of Blacks used the Internet, compared to 60 percent of whites, according to Cyber Dialogue.

such as homegrown artists, in the hundreds in some urban, suburban and rural areas, who are pressing their own CDs and selling them at open mic events, spoken word venues, on consignment at corner stores and so on.

3. The under-the-radar mixtape explosion. Mixtape CDs—unlicensed mass-produced CDs in which a deejay creatively mixes emerging and established rap artist rhyming over unreleased and/or previously published music—have been a phenomenon of hip-hop since at least the 1980s (hence the name). By the mid-1990s mixtape CDs helped break several rappers out of the underground to mainstream hip-hop industry recognition. It was the urban street buzz—generated by their appearance on mixtapes long before securing record deals—that jump-started the careers of artists like DMX, 50 Cent and others. The consumer audience for mixtapes, most certainly in the era before music downloading, was not primarily white suburban youth.

Quantifying anything to do with hip-hop is extremely tricky in most cases and next to impossible in others, in part because so much of hip-hop takes place off the radar. "Corporate America is not sophisticated enough to track the real element buying habits of hip-hop," says hip-hop intellectual Todd Boyd, "so they track what they can quantify. You can't track what's under the radar because no instrument can be created to track it."*

---

*From Todd Boyd's commentary at a Black History Month Forum on hip-hop in a public dialogue with Bakari Kitwana at the University of San Diego, February 17, 2004.

The music industry may be attempting to define the indefinable and will forever be playing catch-up if it intends to document where the hip-hop sales are. When it comes to quantifying mixtapes, it's an especially slippery terrain. Mixtapes in large part rely on copyright infringement, which is illegal, so calculating those sales becomes impossible. "The best way to quantify it is this: there wouldn't be a 50 Cent, there wouldn't be a Jadakiss, if there weren't mixtapes," says Jerry Thompson, codirector of the documentary *Mixtape USA*, which documents one of hip-hop's least-told stories. "Some artists have had their careers made and others resurrected because of mixtapes and there's no way to track mixtape sales because in a lot of cases the deejays are trying to fly under the radar of any organization trying to quantify it."

In the early 1980s mixtapes were for fun and for the love of the art, not financial gain. By the mid-1990s mixtapes had become a business, with the breakthrough of mixtape deejays like New York City's DJ Clue and Houston's DJ Screw. "In the early 1990s it was almost impossible to find mixtapes outside of big cities," says Thompson. But soon mixtapes came to be seen as another viable tool for those trying to break into the industry.

And the real impact of mixtapes can't be comprehended without taking bootlegging into account. "Bootlegging is an important part of the process," says Thompson. "In the mid-1990s if you had a CD burner you probably paid a grand for it. With the availability of CD burners for a fraction of the cost and with the Internet and computer technology, a mixtape CD duplicated 5,000 times by its creator is reaching 20,000 to 30,000 units by the time it's bootlegged." Hip-hop kids across the country are pressing and selling their own CDs, along with a growing cadre of local mixtape deejays. These local deejays in big cities like New York, Miami and Los Angeles, as well as midsize cities like Atlanta and Cleveland, are developing national followings (and the mark they are making in smaller cities is even further off the radar). But it's Internet sales, especially overseas, according to Thompson, that are really helping drive the business. Currently there are scores of Web sites driving sales. Big-name deejays like Kayslay and Green Lantern are doing runs of 10,000 units per CD, according to one record industry executive (who spoke on condition of anonymity, saying that bootlegging is illegal but labels try to use it to their advantage), while lesser-known deejays are moving units anywhere from 1,000 to 5,000 per mixtape. When you consider how regional deejays are putting their own spin on this in addition to unsigned artists selling their own self-published product, the potential sales in this arena are significant and growing.

4. Consumers shopping outside of sales areas. Nielsen-Soundscan categorizes sales based on "low-income" and "high-income" sales areas. But that does not hamper consumers' ability to go outside of sales areas. Americans, across race, class, sex and age, frequent malls in high-income communities. In almost every region of the country, malls in affluent areas have become the shopping locale of choice. Music sales being posted there are not being tracked in terms of race. So even sales posting in a predominantly white, affluent suburb do not always indicate that affluent whites are the only ones buying, especially when significant Black and Latino populations live in close proximity.

The first assumption is that Blacks don't live in high-income areas. Ignored too is the suburbanization of America's economic centers, which began in the late 1960s and early 1970s, further concentrating centers of economic activity like malls in suburban communities. Americans tend to frequent these centers, even urban youth. How many Black kids on the south side and west side of Chicago, for example, shop at Chicago's Watertower Mall, situated in the city's Gold Coast area? The same is true of east side Clevelanders and the suburban Cleveland Beachwood Mall, located in the affluent eastern suburb of Beachwood. These locations don't stop Black kids from shopping there. Neither do they prevent an eighty-year-old white grandmother from buying a hip-hop CD that ends up on a Soundscan data report for a high-income area. Together the Black kid and the eighty-year-old grandmother trump the notion that sales in high-income areas are by definition young, white, suburban males. (This is especially true with CDs, which can quickly sell out in mom-and-pop stores that may lack the buying power of larger corporations, almost forcing consumers to shop elsewhere.)

5. Young Blacks as trendsetters for what's cool. For over a decade, the Philadelphia-based market research company MEE (Motivational, Educational Entertainment) Productions, headed by Ivan Juzang, has been arguing that Black urban youth are trendsetters for youth nationally and internationally. What Black youth are doing today, other ethnic and racial groups will be doing, if not tomorrow, a bit later. In 1992 the company put out its first major breakthrough study, *The MEE Report: Reach-*

ing the Hip-Hop Generation. In 2002 the company released *The National Lifestyle Survey of African American Inner City Youth,* again calling African American youth "the most influential and trendsetting youth market in the world." There is a historical precedent for this—blues, rock and roll and jazz—and hip-hop in this regard isn't vastly different. Black, die-hard hip-hop kids engage anything to do with hip-hop, often a minute before white kids or any other kids further removed from the culture— from the hottest CDs to the latest hip-hop fashion. Given our information age and the mainstreaming of hip-hop, the lag time has decreased. But there is still much hip-hop (music, fashion, language) off the radar that die-hard Black kids are engaging long before white kids, especially those in the hinterlands.

Even when what's hot works its way to the suburbs and rural areas, the Black stamp of approval remains critical. Wendy Day, whose work has taken her deep into the world of hip-hop's mainstream and underground, says this is a critical variable when dealing with hip-hop. "I can tell you as someone who works with independent labels that if you are breaking a record at the street level and you don't have young Black kids buying your record, you will not go anywhere. If there are 2 million white kids out there buying rap records, unless it's legitimized by the Black community, these kids are not buying a damn thing. I guarantee you they are buying whatever people of color they know are listening to." Even David Samuels, author of the *New Republic* piece "The Rap on Rap," concedes that Black kids proportionately buy more hip-hop.

Black kids have been trendsetters in youth culture for so long that this phenomenon is part of the fabric of American society. On the international level, whether in Chile or Brazil, Indonesia, Japan, France, Italy, Ghana or Tanzania, as most emerging hip-hop regions are putting their local stamp on hip-hop, they look to Black American youth as trendsetters. In cases where hip-hop's international audience takes issue with the current crop of young Black hip-hop stars who celebrate materialism and consumer culture, many look to hip-hop's 1980s Black consciousness (Public Enemy, Queen Latifah, KRS-One, Poor Righteous Teachers, X-Clan) as a barometer.

Even Eminem had to get past Black gatekeepers before white hip-hop consumers deemed him good enough. No matter how steeped in hip-hop or marketing finesse, no marketing machine exists that can bypass hip-hop's Black audience. *Are the streets feeling it?* is a constant refrain in the hip-hop industry. Just as Eminem couldn't bypass it, neither can Dizzee Rascal—no matter how many *New York Times* reviews he gets or how many MTV videos are put in heavy rotation. Played out this way, the idea of white primary consumers almost presupposes that white suburban kids are not only major consumers but trendsetters as well, a belief that MTV seems to take at face value, even at times ignoring Black trendsetters.* Dizzee Ras-

---

*MTV has a history of moments when old racial politics–type thinking gets the best of it; it is willing to cash in on Black consumers but unwilling to altogether abandon racist assumptions. MTV gave us Fab Five Freddy's *Yo MTV Raps* in 1988. The same MTV that canceled the show at the first Chicken Little hysteria coming from the music industry that hip-hop sales were falling in 1995. It was MTV that set a standard for acceptable music videos. The same MTV that censored Kanye West's reference to white men in his "Fall Down" video: "Drug dealers buy Jordans, crackheads buy crack/and the white man gets paid off of all of that."

cal's prominent positioning on MTV seems hedged on acceptance of the idea that white kids are buying most of hip-hop and they'll buy him too. No matter how influential MTV is, it cannot bypass that Black stamp of approval. Neither has the hip-hop market yet circumvented Black gatekeepers. The national climate surrounding hip-hop, including telltale moments like these, suggests that we have not yet arrived at the point where Blacks are trendsetters exclusively. They continue to be a significant segment of hip-hop's audience as well.

6. Hip-hop fashion.   Hip-hop fashion is now estimated to be a $2 billion a year business, according to HPD Group, with companies like Rocawear and Ecko each claiming sales of over $300 million a year. Determining how significant a percentage of this audience is white is just as difficult as deciphering the racial breakdown of hip-hop CD sales. That Black representation here is not insignificant but strategically downplayed suggests a pattern that persists when it comes to American corporations and Black youth. Hip-hop fashion is no different. In fact the logic for hip-hop artist–owned fashion companies at their inception was the realization among emerging hip-hop designers that hip-hop kids were a sizable consumer audience for mainstream designers. In the 1980s, "hip-hop fashion" was primarily composed of mainstream designer clothing that hip-hop kids (almost exclusively Blacks and Latinos until the mid-1990s) donned and flipped with their own flavor. Black hip-hop artists made brand names like Lees, Ralph Lauren, Pumas, Filas, Addidas, Timberland or Tommy Hilfiger must-have products for hip-hop kids. So complete was hip-hop's appropriation of

Timberland that in 1994 the company's chief operating officer issued a public statement reassuring customers that it wasn't abandoning its base for the "urban" market.

Hip-hop stars' awareness that Black kids were contributing significantly to these companies' bottom lines sparked the trend of hip-hop artist footwear and clothing companies. That, and a healthy dose of disrespect from these companies when artists sought to build business relationships in order to cash in on the free publicity they were providing in rap lyrics and more. Those who find it far-fetched for Blacks to be significant consumers should consider the case of the French cognac maker Courvoisier. The boost that Busta Rhymes's song "Pass the Courvoisier" gave to the company simply can't be denied. Accompanying and following the success of the song, sales skyrocketed. According to the *New York Times* (September 2, 2002) sales of the liquor increased by 4.5 percent in the first quarter of 2002 and double digits months later. Currently African Americans represent 70 percent of Courvoisier's U.S. sales.*

In the context of the old racial politics, Blacks individually and collectively continue to be undervalued as consumers when convenient. Their impact is downplayed both when it comes to hip-hop music sales and the various ways hip-hop is affecting the marketplace.

---

*Likewise, Cadillac Escalade and clothing company Dolce Gabanna don't mind giving artists free products for their videos and awards show appearances, but they haven't shown a tendency to give them a piece of the pie. Busta Rhymes wasn't paid to write the song, although the *New York Times* reported that the company struck a promotional deal later with Busta's management company, Violator.

7. Hip-hop's influence in the lives of Black youth. Built into the assumption that white suburban male teens are the primary buying audience for hip-hop is the implication that they are the primary listening audience as well. Sure, it is statistically possible that, given their representation in the overall U.S. population, young whites are hip-hop's primary consumers. But it is also statistically possible that young Blacks, given the profound and pervasive influence of hip-hop culture in their lives, could well be the primary buying audience. Given the profound impact of hip-hop in their lives, that young Blacks are a significant listening audience is hardly debatable. Of course, hip-hop is a primary influence among today's youth across the board, including countless white youth who feel alienated from mainstream American life and find refuge in hip-hop. But it is difficult to dismiss the sense of urgency among young Blacks, especially since the music originated in Black urban communities and young whites have begun to pay attention in substantial numbers only recently. This music and culture speaks to the importance of the new Black youth culture to this generation.

Hip-hop has a wide range of white listeners, what Marc Spiegler called concentric circles (see Chapter 2). At the innermost circle are whites who feel a similar sense of urgency—a minority of hip-hop's white audience. In Black communities among hip-hop listeners, you probably find the reverse in terms of a concentric circles formation. The vast majority of Black listeners are those who feel locked out of the American mainstream—economically, socially and politically. Their job options are extremely limited (minimum wage, no-benefit

employment or the military for those who lack college education, or no job at all as unemployment continues to skyrocket
among young Blacks). In hip-hop they see a place for themselves in American society where they are centered and hold
both power and influence, whether embracing the status quo
or opposing it. These dynamics are the driving force behind
hip-hop's cultural movement and emerging political movement. The economic, political and social realities pervasive in
hip-hop, even at its most conformist, have captured the imagination of young Blacks across the country.

In the absence of social intervention in the lives of abandoned young people, hip-hop has filled the void. And indeed if
hip-hop is a culture—and it is—it has created a political, spiritual and economic philosophy that reinforces its right to exist.
Consequently we see young Blacks making a connection to the
larger society most effectively when hip-hop is the bridge.
Where the Black church is failing to reach young people, enter
hip-hop ministries to bridge the gap. Where prisons have become the final solution for American youth and have failed to
rehabilitate them, hip-hop there has become an answer, as a
locale for some artists to jump-start their careers, moving
them from the underground economy to the mainstream one.

Where schools are failing to reach young Blacks, the hip-
hop arts via various hip-hop collectives across the country are
emerging as a valuable point of reference. By connecting to
what they know in hip-hop, kids are able to make the leap to
what before seemed distant, foreign, in art, history, language
and so on. For example, nothing in recent history has paral-

leled the explosive interest in poetry among young people—
not just reading but writing their own—as has hip-hop. Hip-
hop has inspired a generation once deemed "lost," and young
Blacks are pursuing mainstream careers related to hip-hop as a
result (producers, business, law, publicity, etc.).

This also brings to mind the attendance of African American and Latino youth at hip-hop political events, where economic, social and political issues are raised. At the twenty-six
hip-hop summits that took place nationwide during the 18
months leading up to the 2004 election, Black and Latino
youth were the primary audience (over 95 percent). It should
be clear by now that hip-hop as a Black youth subculture has
a profound influence on the lives of Black youth. Black youth
are being heavily influenced by the culture and certainly they
are listening to, buying and engaging with the music as well.
They aren't only listening to the music; as part of the culture,
it's become a major force in their lives.

From the Corporate Boardroom to the Ivory Tower

Why is this discussion about hip-hop's primary listening and/
or buying audience important in the first place? Why should
race still matter when it comes to hip-hop, especially as a new
racial politics is emerging among the younger generations?
Ultimately what matters is not *who* is buying the music, but
why this detail has been overemphasized when its validity
rests on such shaky ground. There would be nothing wrong
with claiming that white kids are hip-hop's primary audience

if that were indeed the case. But what's at stake if white kids are not hip-hop's primary audience and we accept the myth? The overwhelming message here is that Blacks are not a significant variable in a music they created and a music of which Black culture is the very foundation. The implication is that, as David Samuels wrote in 1991, Blacks, over a decade later, aren't the driving force behind the music, neither on the creative and business ends nor on the consumption side.

Jason Middleton and Roger Beebe, in an article entitled "The Racial Politics of Hybridity and Neo-Eclecticism in Contemporary Popular Music" (in *Popular Music*, 2002, pp. 159–172), suggest that the mainstreaming of hip-hop manifested itself in the early 2000s trend of white rock-rap bands or white rock and rap musicians using hip-hop and its images but divorcing them from their Black origins. They refer to this trend interchangeably as "decontextualization," "displacing race," "expunging Black signifiers" and "erasing the Black cultural context." In a similar vein, Bill Yousman in the November 2003 issue of *Communication Theory*, in a piece entitled "Blackophilia and Blackophobia: White Youth, the Consumption of Rap Music and White Supremacy," writes,

Although early adopters of rap music among White youth may thus have been motivated by rebellious impulses, as more and more White youth embrace rap music, the trend takes on a momentum of its own and provides a common sort of cultural vocabulary for youths from all cultural backgrounds. It thus becomes a cultural imperative for many

White youth to embrace rap music in order to fit in with their peer group. (p. 366)

Yousman argues that white kids are accepting hip-hop culture as their own only to an extent. Further, Yousman believes that it is the old racial politics in the form of "white supremacy" (i.e., Black kids selling Black images of Black criminality and inferiority and white kids buying them to reinforce their superiority) that is the real driving force behind white suburban teens' desire to consume hip-hop, not an authentic appreciation of Black culture. Comparing white youth appropriation of hip-hop to nineteenth-century white minstrel performers in Blackface, Yousman writes,

White youth adoption of Black cultural forms in the 21st century is also a performance, one that allows Whites to contain their fears and animosities toward Blacks through rituals not of ridicule, as in previous eras, but of adoration. Thus, although the motives behind their performance may initially appear to be different, the act is still a manifestation of White supremacy, albeit a White supremacy that is in crisis and disarray, rife with confusion and contradiction.

Cultural critic Stanley Crouch and many other Black baby boomers point to this in their assessment of hip-hop as "a modern minstrel show." Yousman drives the point home by arguing that white youth fascination with hip-hop culture coexists with "the continuing manifestations of white youth

resistance to programs that challenge institutional racism."
My belief is that rather than being resistant, many white hip-
hop kids have yet to realize that it is up to them to create such
programs. Yet it is impossible to dismiss critics like Yousman
given the glaring moments when hip-hop as a pop culture
phenomenon does indeed evoke old stereotypes about Blacks
(as criminals and oversexed, for example). The pervasiveness
of these stereotypes, rooted in the old racial politics, has not
stopped young whites from consuming hip-hop that contains
them.

If Yousman, Beebe and Middleton are even partially correct, then this unspoken but growing trend among mass audiences to expunge Blackness from hip-hop is reinforced by the
myth of hip-hop's primary white audience. The trend is
emerging at the same time that hip-hop studies is entering
the academy. Will it ensure that hip-hop scholars who are
white fare better than those who are Black?

For example, Black youth who've grown up in and are defined by hip-hop and go on to pursue graduate degrees focused on hip-hop report resistance from Black and white
professors alike. White (and honorary white) graduate students doing the same report little or no resistance. This is not
a hip-hop conspiracy theory. Students report various reasons
for their mentors' response to hip-hop, such as older Black
scholars who tell younger ones that hip-hop as a field of study
is too limiting. However, the result is a restricted circle of
scholars emerging at a time when hip-hop is making its debut
as an intellectual line of inquiry. Such scholars will ultimately
lay the groundwork for the discipline.

The process brings to mind a question similar to the one that was raised when Black studies came into existence in 1968: What is the role of hip-hop studies and how will it empower its practitioners? Why raid hip-hop for ideas to fuel a handful of academic careers, while giving nothing back to the culture, its creators or practitioners?

Given hip-hop's influence on American youth, any intellectual inquiry into hip-hop should be actively exploring ways of empowering youth, with young people of color prominently in the picture. If hip-hop studies fail to do this, if hip-hop intellectuals allow it to become about individual careers and endless pontificating, the result could be the following: (1) the emergence of white hip-hop critics (far removed from the culture) farther out ahead in the field than Black critics (closer to the culture), placing their stamp on the groundwork for how hip-hop will be defined and the history of hip-hop culture in all its manifestations will be recorded and remembered for the ages; and (2) alongside them, and often behind them in the wings, will sit Black and brown academics so steeped in academic jargon that their analysis of hip-hop will do little to intervene in the lives of youth now empowered by it. Will these become the ultimate authorities on hip-hop? The number of courses being taught exclusively about or including some aspect of hip-hop at colleges and universities across the country grows daily (over 700 at last count). What is being taught? Who is teaching it? What will be the result?

These critical questions are directly linked to the unsubstantiated myth of hip-hop's primary audience. And this arena of definitions is the real place where the battle for hip-hop's soul is being waged. It is a battle that will define the history of hip-hop, the place of Blacks and browns in the United States at the start of the twenty-first century, and also whether or not this generation through hip-hop will live up to its promise to change America. If white hip-hop kids ignore hip-hop's history and do not resist the temptation to reproduce the old racial politics, we will have lost a beautiful democratic momentum set in motion by American youth, one that has the vision and the capacity to leave the old racial politics on the pages of history where it belongs.

PART TWO

Answers
From W.E.B. Du Bois to Chuck D

The year 2003 marked the hundredth anniversary of the publication of W.E.B. Du Bois's *The Souls of Black Folk.* To commemorate the occasion, Running Press released *Reconsidering the Souls of Black Folk: Thoughts on the Groundbreaking Classic Work of W.E.B. Du Bois,* a book coauthored by famed jazz critic and syndicated columnist Stanley Crouch and journalist and historian Playthell Benjamin. As part of the book's promotion, the two appeared at Studio Museum in Harlem on April 2, 2003 (the event was later televised on C-Span's *Book TV*).

Bringing together the highly opinionated, self-righteous and take-no-prisoners personas of Stanley Crouch and Playthell Benjamin was bound to be explosive. The format allowed each coauthor to comment at length on his contribution to the book, followed by a question-and-answer period. The forum was a perfect example of what a serious intellectual exchange should

look like: accomplished, headstrong intellectuals, both impro-
vising and building off each other's insights.

Hip-hop reared its head several times during the dialogue.
The first moment came when Stanley Crouch spoke about
the impact of Du Bois's book on race relations then and now.
"The idea of a Negro with a brain, that's still an idea that's kind
of locked in a cage. And rappers don't help that either." At that
point he was interrupted by someone from the audience who
took offense at the hip-hop put-down. Benjamin, still focused
strictly on Du Bois, let it slide. Crouch continued, "You can say
that if you want to, but I look at MTV. You turn that on and if
you think these Negroes got brains, you're crazy. . . . *The Souls
of Black Folk* was an intellectual atom bomb."

The second instance came about an hour and fifteen minutes into the program, during the Q&A.

Crouch said, "I was talking to some guy in Canada and he
said, 'Well one of the things we have to say about rap is its word
driven.'" Crouch continued:

> I said, 'But that's not why you like it, though.' He said, 'What
> do you mean that's not why I like it?' I said, 'You like it and the
> rest of you white people like it for one very specific reason,
> and that is whenever you read those lyrics, as they're called,
> you always know, or assume, that you are superior to the
> Negro who wrote them.' That is not something anybody is
> every going to feel about reading *The Souls of Black Folk*.

It's not hard to disagree with Stanley Crouch. But it's not
easy to dismiss him completely either. "There may be some

truth to that," Benjamin said, easing in. But this time he didn't let Stanley's transgressions against hip-hop pass unchallenged.

My daughter is a renaissance woman. . . . *She* likes hip-hop, loves it. . . . My kids grew up in Harlem. They're twins and the worst trouble I ever had out of them was getting them to keep their rooms clean. And *they* love hip-hop. My son don't listen to *nothing but hip-hop*. . . and as a consequence I listen to it and have written some very intelligent essays about it too. Ms. Green's son, Talib Kweli, he's a real poet as is Rakim. Nas is a street poet of sorts. And I can go on. . . . Read my section in the book called 'Some Antecedents of *Souls*.' Look at my in-depth discussion of German classical music, I mean in-depth. I know about music. I have a real serious music education. My aunt was a classically trained pianist who also played rag-time and everything else. Her brother and my grandfather could play anything on the piano. My aunt was a choir master. I sang all the choral classics coming up. I was singing in du-wop groups when I was coming up. I played drums in a jazz band. I play congas right now. I've been playing Afro-Cuban music for 40 years. I've played with Mongo Santa Maria, Willie Bobo and everybody else and *I* like hip-hop. Enuf said.

And so a consideration of W.E.B. Du Bois's *The Souls of Black Folk*, a book that's remained in print for one hundred years and, according to Benjamin and Crouch, has influenced every generation since its publication, ended with a discussion of the significance of hip-hop and race.

Indeed, hip-hop has profound things to tell us about race, if we dare to listen. Its pull is irresistible, its range infinite. It rattles our wildest assumptions about race, even as it indulges and bears out every stereotype imaginable. It is a product of America at the dawn of the twenty-first century that instills in nearly everyone, from its most strident opponent to its fiercest defender, an argumentative voice, bidding us to collectively give chase. Like W.E.B. Du Bois's *The Souls of Black Folk*, hip-hop's impact cuts across generations, race and class. For now, its mission, much like that of *Souls*, prevails. What rapper Chuck D in 1988 (on the single "Don't Believe the Hype") put succinctly: "Reach the bourgeois and rock the boulevard."

4

Wankstas, Wiggers and Wannabes

Hip-Hop, Film and White Boyz in the Hood

And I just do not got the patience
To deal with these cocky caucasians
Who think I'm some wigger who just tries to be black
Cause I talk with an accent, and grab on my balls,
So they always keep askin the same fuckin questions
What school did I go to, what hood I grew up in.
                                    —Eminem, "The Way I Am"

As hip-hop was on the fast track to becoming a force in mainstream American popular culture by the mid-1990s, its presence inevitably became felt in film as well. Much of the 1990s were dominated by Black gangsta films—slice-of-life, coming-of-age stories of young Black urban reality, such as *Boyz N the Hood*, *New Jack City*, and *Menace II Society*. Lingering in the shadows of gangsta-thug glory were a handful of films that commented on the growing influence of Black youth culture in the lives of white American youth. The brow raisers *Bulworth* (1998) and *Black and White* (1999), as well as the misunderstood *Malibu's Most Wanted* (2003), all addressed the extent to which hip-hop had come to permeate the mainstream.

Borrowing from their Black gangsta cousins, these films featured big-name rappers (such as Snoop Dogg, Queen Latifah and Raekwon) and hip-hop-dominant soundtracks. At the same time most of these movies faced marketing difficulties because they seemed to be promoting stereotypes of African Americans, a criticism also heaped on Black gangsta films. But the films tell us much more than their own promoters say about them.* They dare to delve into unconventional arenas by (1) suggesting that race relations were changing beneath the radar and hip-hop was playing a role, (2) dissecting the new realities of race in America and (3) challenging the old racial politics. Rather than be vilified, these films should be applauded for breaking new ground. More than anything else, they have begun the difficult work of initiating one of the most honest public dialogues around race since the 1970s. Not just a discussion of Black issues and identity or white angst and resentment against America's minorities, these films all teach us something about this space and time called

---

*The simplistic description on the DVD jacket for *Malibu's Most Wanted*, for example, didn't venture outside the gates of the old racial politics: "A rich white wannabe rapper gets a dose of reality when forced to spend a day in the hood."

hip-hop where Black youth culture and white youth culture converge.

In the framework of the old racial politics, white engagement with Black culture is cast as infatuation and generally deemed a "cultural safari," and nothing more. But as noted in the previous chapter, nothing could be further from the truth. The terms "wanksta, wigger and wannabe" all defy and exaggerate reality.

> *Wanksta*: a wannabe gangsta. An expression popularized by rapper 50 Cent to describe a gangsta wannabe.
>
> *Wigger*: a young white who wants desperately to be down with hip-hop, who identifies more strongly with Black culture than white. (What's disturbing about this expression is its racist implications: if white kids down with hip-hop are "wiggers," what does that make Black kids down with hip-hop?)
>
> *Wannabe*: someone uncomfortable being himself or herself and fanatically trying to be someone else. Long used in Black American colloquial language to describe an outsider aping insider behavior and popularized among the younger generation by the 1988 Spike Lee film *School Daze*.

Each of these terms relative to white youth and hip-hop is key to understanding the clash between the old racial politics and the new racial politics brought closer to fruition by what cultural critic Nelson George calls a "hip-hop America."

> It [*Hip-Hop America*] is about the society-altering collision that has taken place during the last two decades between black

youth culture and the mass media, about the discovering (maybe hijacking) of black youths as creators and consumers . . . how advertisers, magazines, MTV, fashion companies, beer and soft drink manufacturers, and multimedia conglomerates like Time-Warner have embraced hip hop as a way to reach not just black young people but all young people. It's an extension of the record biz concept of crossover, which itself was a byproduct of Motown success; at some point Run-DMC became the Supremes. But in the 90s with more sophisticated marketing techniques and more complicated motions across old racial boundaries, the payoffs are bigger than Berry Gordy could cash in on. (*Hip-Hop America*, p. ix)

In the confines of the old racial politics, these were among a handful of ways in which white youth could engage Black youth culture—not natural but abnormal or even vulgar.

These films spin the old ways of thinking about race on their head. Films that fit the "wanksta, wigger and wannabe" description deftly take on four issues central to the phenomenon of white kids engaging hip-hop culture. The first is parody. Are white kids belittling or celebrating Black culture by engaging hip-hop? Second, appropriation. Are white kids stealing Black culture or retailoring it to their reality? Third, the generation gap. What role does global economics play—relative to how work and pop culture are defined—in forging a wider generational divide? Fourth, interracial dating. As a major preoccupation in the history of American race relations, how does this generation view and engage interracial dating? Even though a new racial politics is unfolding, how do they navigate the presence of the old racial politics?

James Toback's 1999 film *Black and White* was one of the first attempts to provide white kids' own perspective on their seeming fascination with hip-hop and Black youth culture. One of the important elements of the movie, which Toback identifies in a DVD promotional interview for the film, was to avoid preaching. Instead, his vision was to simply present a glimpse into "a world" and allow viewers to draw their own conclusions. "It's not a movie that presents two or three viewpoints and says you should subscribe to this," he said. "It just shows a world and lets you feel your way into it, observe it, watch it, reject it, accept it, respond to it." However, this "glimpse alone" approach has its limitations.

As the film presents viewers with unfiltered access to this world, a focused plot, among other things, gets lost. *Black and White* is the story of a drug dealer, Rich Bowers, his crew and their attempt to transition from a street underworld lifestyle into the hip-hop industry—although for much of the film Rich seems to be balancing both. The film has several subplots. The first concerns a group of white prep school kids fascinated by Black youth culture who are the subject of a documentary on white kids obsessed with hip-hop. Another subplot involves Rich's childhood friend Dean, a college ballplayer who takes a bribe from an undercover police detective, Mark Clear. The detective hopes that by entrapping Dean, he can get him to sell out Rich. Meanwhile the detective (portrayed by Ben Stiller) has a partially explained past with

Dean's girlfriend Greta, a white graduate student. The third subplot is about Will, a white kid who's estranged from his father, who happens to be the district attorney.

Will has immersed himself in the hood and is working hard to be down with Rich Bowers. Will's younger brother is Marty. Marty is among the crew of white preppy kids, as well as Charlie and Raven, two white girls who are intimately involved with Rich. Dean's decision to sell out Rich leads Greta into a sexual relationship with Rich and leads Rich to put a hit on Dean. Will is the hit man and with his father as the DA, Greta as the former girlfriend of Mark Clear, the detective, the connections between these subplots are gradually revealed.

But not without a few obvious speed bumps. The white kids involved are exclusively from upper-middle-class backgrounds. The perspectives of middle-class and poor whites engaging hip-hop are missing from this film. Also, the voices of the handful of white kids we meet in the film are superficial. What they have to say about hip-hop and cross-racial interaction is stifled, almost programmed. More complex issues of Black and white youth engagement via hip-hop, such as the generation gap, culture banditry, identity, cultural authenticity and exclusiveness, even when mentioned, are skimmed over. One of the film's greatest obstacles is that the white kids on screen themselves are not engaging hip-hop culture. They are strictly observers, for the most part mimicking Black youth behavior. Whether Charlie is engaging the documentary maker, her parents or her Black friends, you never get the sense that the hip-hop-laced identity she's assuming is authentically hers. She's always grasping at straws. Also, whenever white kids and Black kids interact, rather than appearing natural and fluid, the film is in a continuing state of surprise; surprise at the interaction, surprise that white kids would love hip-hop in the first place, surprise that white kids would emulate Black youth culture or admire Black kids. A scene in which the rappers meet with filmmaker and music video director Brett Ratner to talk about their music video is the best example of this. Because of moments like these, the film never goes subsurface. Likewise, the ways white and Black youth engage each other via hip-hop gets lost in *Black and White*.

Bulworth, written and directed by Warren Beatty, hit theaters in 1998. A film about a United States senator on the last leg of a reelection campaign as well as on the verge of a nervous breakdown, *Bulworth* includes a subplot that offers a piercing perspective of hip-hop's impact on mainstream American culture. Throughout the film, the hip-hop subplot is never out of focus and always threatens to take center stage. Senator Jay Bulworth is a Democrat, but, just like most of today's Democrats, he's veered eerily close to being a Republican—though he still dons Democratic clothing. He's haunted by the social justice roots of his early days, which he, now a career politician, betrayed a long time ago. (He periodically refers to his progressive 1960s activism, including his association with the Black Panther Party for Self-Defense.) He hates himself and the ways he and others like him kiss up to corporate power. He knows the system isn't working for the majority of Americans, but he plays the game to his own end anyway—until he suffers a mental breakdown. In breakdown mode he turns cynical and resolves to do battle against all the contradictions he's come to represent. To do so he uses hip-hop as his medium.

His final deal in Congress is to push through a bill in favor of the insurance industry, in exchange for hefty policies that will benefit his family in the event of his death, which he knows is coming: he's hired a hit man to put him out of his misery. Along the way, he meets a handful of young Blacks who remind him of the human face behind the statistics. He's also reminded that his own life is worth living. But before he gets that far his cynicism leads him to using rap as the mouthpiece for articulating the hypocrisies of the American political scene. To do this he doesn't enlist the support of actual rappers, as some real-life politicians have recently done. Instead, he starts to rap himself in his speeches as well as in media appearances.

To be sure, *Bulworth* is not an attempt to unveil a sixty-something white guy who successfully appropriates hip-hop. When he's rapping, the senator stands out like a sore thumb because he's supposed to. But while Senator Bulworth may not get all the nuances of hip-hop culture, he certainly gets why its message resonates with youth across race:

> White boy busting ass til they put him in his grave. He ain't gotta be Black to be living like a slave. Rich people have always stayed on top by dividing white people from colored people but white people have more in common with colored people than they do with rich people.

The film suggests that kids who love hip-hop, especially the Black kids who birthed it, understand that U.S. public policy has stacked the deck against them—in education, policing, incarceration, housing, economic infrastructure, jobs and more. Hip-hop is the voice that speaks to this reality. This theme recurs in the film's scenes, dialogue and most strikingly in Senator Bulworth's rhymes, like this one from a television interview:

Middle class getting poorer. Rich getting richer . . . public schools that are a nightmare. Where did all the good jobs go? My contributors make more profits hiring kids in Mexico. What we used to call America is going down the drain. A million brothers in prison. Constitution supposed to give them an equal chance. But they speak for the richest 20 percent while pretending they're defending the meek.

The senator's use of hip-hop to articulate America's political ills is no coincidence.

Although hip-hop (its messages of resistance and its anti-Black and antiwomen representations) is ever present, you don't find young whites and Blacks coming together via hip-hop in this film. Instead, baby boomer Senator Bulworth appropriates the voice of the younger generation to make a point to his peers, one that young people already get. *Bulworth* breaks new ground in successfully portraying hip-hop as the most viable arena for correcting America's unresolved race relations. In *Bulworth*, hip-hop is a vehicle, a tool deployed to shock, perplex and force people to reflect. But as hip-hop is not the immediate subject and young whites down with it are nowhere to be found here, the film hints at far more questions about white kids and hip-hop than it answers.

It would be nearly four years before a film emerged with the right mix of humor, candidness and cultural confidence to deliver. *Malibu's Most Wanted* (2003), in its sophisticated treatment of the issues, with the questions it raises and the answers it provides, outdistances both *Black and White* and *Bulworth*. Starring generation X comedian Jamie Kennedy, the comedic film centers around Bradley (Brad), a.k.a. B-Rad, an aspiring rapper who's come of age in Malibu, California. Clearly secure in an upper-middle-class enclave, complete with servants and every gadget imaginable, he's a modern-day Richie Rich. But where there is no problem, leave it to America's superrich to invent one. B-Rad's crisis is that he's a virtual Black kid in a young white body. He raps, though his skill leaves much to the imagination. He also talks the talk and walks the walk of a Black kid from America's most concrete-filled jungle. Problem is, he's never been to the hood. To add insult to injury, he doesn't even have Black friends.

Meanwhile, B-Rad's father, Bill Gluckman (played by Ryan O'Neal), is in the midst of a gubernatorial campaign. B-Rad's "acting Black" threatens to sabotage it—over Tom Gibbsons's dead body. Played by Blair Underwood, Gibbsons is Gluckman's campaign manager and arguably B-Rad's opposite: he's a white man in a Black man's body. Ironically, it is Gibbsons who perceives B-Rad as the only obstacle to his candidate's victory. Willing to do whatever it takes to win, he concocts a bizarre scheme to get B-Rad out of the way by any means necessary. He will hire two Black actors to escort B-Rad to the hood and, by introducing him firsthand to the thug life to which he thinks B-Rad aspires, scare B-Rad straight (or, rather, "white"). Oh, and one more thing. His Black tour guides aren't from the hood, hence the acting is just that, an act. So, here we have two Black guys acting "Black" to try to render "white" a white guy perceived to be acting "Black." This comedic value allows the film to launch a sophisticated sneak attack.

Parody and Appropriation

Films that fit the wanksta, wigger and wannabe mold unquestionably and inevitably parody Black youth *popular* culture. The question *Malibu's Most Wanted* poses is: When does Black youth culture end and the packaged imitation Black youth culture begin? The distortions of Black youth culture that get played out every day from Black gangsta films to music videos are *Malibu's* fodder.

At the film's start, this parody comes straight out of the gate *Scary Movie*–style as the film mimics a similarly narrated scene from the Black gangsta film *Menace II Society*. The narrator in *Menace* explains why and how the central character, O-Dog, is a product of his environment, a subject without agency or free will. Ditto for B-Rad. Just as *Menace* portrays gun toting and thugging as business as usual in the hood, in *Malibu's Most Wanted* we get a narration of how Malibu, sarcastically, isn't that different: bag ladies (women shopping at the mall), crime, drugs, "big ballers" and gun toters. On the surface, this parody is offensive, as is B-Rad's exaggerated Black ghetto accent. ("Dis our mall," he says describing the various facets of his hood in the first scene.) Most often, however, the jokes aren't at the expense of Black American culture but, rather, those aspects of hip-hop that have become parodies of themselves—from Black kids use of the n-word to rap music videos' mindless and endless parade of booty shaking, scantily clad women and misogynistic behavior. Complete with references to bitches and hos, all are targets in this film.

What better way to highlight the distortions than to lump much of this mayhem into one scene? In an attempt to help out on the campaign, rather than continue to undermine it by being himself, B-Rad is asked to create a banner and perform an uplifting rap song that celebrates women at one of his father's campaign stops. Coming straight out of B-Rad's pop culture hip-hop playbook, the banner reads, "Gluckman's down with the bitches and hos." The song he performs makes similar references. Additionally, true to his mainstream hip-hop upbringing, his stage props are rump-shaking, half-naked young women.

That many white kids who appropriate Black youth culture rely heavily on the popular culture distortions is something that *Malibu's Most Wanted* gets right. It's an important element of the white kids and hip-hop phenomenon that gets lost in other films. In *Bulworth* and in the more recent *Bringing Down the House*, whites' impersonation of Black youth culture is extreme. Indeed, this exaggeration is by design. But in these films, it is baby boomers who assume a Black style of dress and affected speech and appear to mock young Blacks, if not young whites enamored with Black culture. Senator Bulworth sheds his suit and tie and "dresses up" in a young Black man's clothes instead. Overhearing Blacks talking, he works their vernacular into his colloquial language. In *Bringing Down the House*, the white Sanderson loses his suit and tie and dons a hip-hop uniform of baggy jeans, throwback jersey and a skully. His buddy Eugene, in an attempt to impress Charlene (Queen Latifah), adopts Black vernacular as well. More than an act, he's attempting to be a part of Charlene's world. His efforts seem sincere enough. By contrast, the young preppy white kids in *Black and White* are only half serious. They want one foot in their comfort zone—white elite circles—a few toes dabbling in a white youth cool and a few others in their interaction with a handful of Black friends. Toback attempts to take us to a world beyond strictly vulgar imitation when he gets to the end of the film and makes projections about where the white kids are six months later: Raven is pursuing another young Black male love interest, Charlie is just confused and Will is coaching a basketball team. The film's ending suggests that something more than parody is at work. But neither *Black and White* nor *Bulworth* effectively highlights, as *Malibu's Most Wanted* does, that sometimes white youth who rely exclusively on media representations of hip-hop are appropriating distorted representations of Black youth culture, not Black youth culture itself.

Malibu's Most Wanted also distinguishes itself by going the distance to reveal that even though at times there may be an overemphasis on acting "Black," white kids who love hip-hop are not simply making fun of Black people—neither are they parasitically appropriating Black culture. There are distinctions of parody. This film makes fun of Black people even as it celebrates the impact of Black culture on white America. At the same time, there is a difference between "culture banditry," appropriation that comes in the form of an outsider ripping off another culture, and "acknowledged appropriation," where the outsider emulates a culture *and* redefines it, while acknowledging its roots. In many cases, white kids' love for hip-hop, contrary to popular opinion, is more than just acting "Black." Nothing brings this point home more effectively than the way the film juxtaposes B-Rad to a pair of young Black men whose task in the film is to act "Black." B-Rad is one part exaggeration and ninety-nine parts true to himself. The actors, on the other hand, manufacture their Black identities. Ultimately the film asks, Who is Blacker? The Black suburban guys who have to learn how to act "Black" in order to scare B-Rad "white" or B-Rad, who, even though he's acquired a sense of Blackness, has an identity that is more authentically his own?

In absorbing aspects of Black youth culture, largely via popular culture, young whites have created their own subculture. This can be observed in part in the accent that B-Rad affects in the film, which is at times a "Black" accent but at others a distinctive white hip-hop kid accent. We see a similar manifestation of this in the character Charlie in *Black and White*. Interestingly, Charlie wants to immerse herself in Black culture but realizes she is just in it and not of it. "I want to be Black," she says in class discussion in response to her teacher's questions regarding youth and identity. "I want to get into the hip-hop thing. I want to go there." Charlie's desire is to be down with hip-hop and Black boys, not so much to be Black, and most certainly not be a Black girl. She aspires to engage hip-hop as a race-free identity, but at the point in the film where we meet her she hasn't yet arrived:

> "I'm a little kid," she continues. "Kids go through phases. I like it now and I'm gonna stand up for it and be like I'm into hip-hop. When it comes down to it—I'll be over it soon. But for right now, while I'm in school and I've got comfort and I'm okay and all my friends are into it, I can go hang out with them, I can go and be a part of that. I can do whatever I want. I'm a kid in America."

Toback put it this way: "[*Black and White*] suggests that identity is fluid. One can make of one's self another self from other selves."

This idea of hip-hop as another space that is neither Black nor white is what actress Elizabeth Regen suggested when she was interviewed by the *New York Times* (September 28, 2003, Arts, p. 24) for an article entitled "The Blackest White Girl on TV." Both quoting and paraphrasing Regen, who plays the role of a Black-acting white woman on the NBC sitcom *Whoopi*, Baz Driesinger writes:

> "I don't want Rita to be mistaken for having been seriously influenced by the African American culture," she [Regen] says. "She's influenced by hip-hop culture," which Ms. Regen sees as "made up of music and language and art and ethnicities all mixed together. So anybody of any race can identify with it."

In suggesting that hip-hop is not exclusively a Black thing, Regen draws too wide a distinction between hip-hop and Black American culture. Of course we should not take her uninformed opinion as hard truth. She's correct that Black American culture and hip-hop aren't always interchangeable. But she's dead wrong in suggesting that hip-hop is interchangeable with a hodgepodge of cultures. Hip-hop is a subculture of Black youth culture. Those who suggest it isn't are confused, misled, trying to appropriate Black youth culture or too culturally arrogant to realize that they are appropriating.

Although she lacks a language for articulating it, Regen seems to be suggesting that white kids down with hip-hop are evolving their own speech, style and so on, which come out of and are influenced by Black youth culture but do not mimic it. Instead, young white hip-hop kids are in some ways creating a distinctive white hip-hop subculture. Similarly Japanese, Indonesians, Brazilians, French and Israeli rappers are evolving a hip-hop that borrows from U.S.-based hip-hop but isn't just aping Black American culture. Rather they are embracing Black youth culture, making aspects of the subculture their own and out of that place where both cultures meet, emitting their interpretation of hip-hop. At some crucial point this means redefining hip-hop through their eyes.*

---

*Consider the Israeli rapper Subliminal, whose lyrics critics have been described as fascist, pro-Zionist and anti-Palestinian. As part of an oppressor class appropriating hip-hop, which has historically represented the oppressed, this is appropriation of the likes hip-hop has never seen.

Generation Gap

Next, these films go beyond parody and appropriation to examine a central phenomenon to any discussion of white kids and hip-hop: the generation gap between baby boomer parents and their children (generation X and the millennium generation). How the globalization of the economy is affecting American life is central to this generation gap. Two things are at work here. First, parents are working longer hours and spending less time with their children. Second, pop culture is filling the void. It is a pop culture steeped as much in the new global economics as the work-til-you-drop world that consumes today's parents. The result is a distance between parents and children. More and more, popular culture, including hip-hop, is filling the void.

In *Malibu's Most Wanted* B-Rad's parents take him to a psychiatrist to find out what's going wrong in his brain to make him act "Black." Never one to hold back, B-Rad pours it on. The psychiatrist describes his condition as "gangsta envy" and asks him when he first started feeling different. B-Rad recalls several incidents from his childhood when his parents weren't around and hip-hop was. The film then takes us through blasts of B-Rad's past filled with pop culture references, absent parents and Black servants influencing him as much as or more than his parents—but not as much as pop culture. The first is when he's left alone with the maid. She's cleaning and listening to Run DMC on headphones. The phone rings and she puts down the Walkman and goes to answer it. Three-year-old B-Rad picks up her headphones and hears hip-hop for the first time.

The second incident comes when his parents go out and leave B-Rad to watch television. He quickly surfs to *The Fresh Prince of Bel-Air*, the 1990s sitcom starring Will Smith. Part of the point here is that global economics has changed the way culture is transmitted. Our parents' overemphasis on the paper chase, which for us is articulated via pop culture television, film and music, has consequences. In the information age, the question is: At what point does parenting end and marketing begin? Our culture's obsession with consumerism has consequences. When consumerism is your God, parental whims take a backseat to popular culture. While parents are paper chasing, so are others. Some of these others are marketing and selling any- and everything to our very own children, including hip-hop via popular culture.

Finally, the generation gap persists to a large degree because parents can't distinguish between hip-hop and American pop culture. Distinctions must be drawn between hip-hop as it's packaged for consumption and the local, off-the-radar culture of hip-hop that young people live and engage every day. The old racial politics isn't equipped with a language for deciphering these subtleties. Some white kids are just along for a pop culture ride; some white kids who are down with hip-hop don't fully "get" Black culture; and sometimes there are even more layers of culture to work through, such as prison culture and street culture that have worked their way into popular hip-hop culture to the extent that they seem indistinguishable. In the case of B-Rad all three conditions are true.

In *Black and White,* far more than in *Bulworth,* we get hints of this. The distance between Charlie and her parents, just like the distance between Marty and Will and their father, seems to be run-of-the-mill teen angst and rebellion that is unrelated to new global realities. We don't get the sense that the gap is a real one—just imagined. Will and Marty seem ready to make the peace and come into the world of their father, who doesn't attempt to understand the intricacies of a new America where white and Black youth cultures blend together. And Charlie is aware that she's in a phase that she'll outgrow. The film doesn't go beyond an elementary level in approaching these intricacies of the generation gap. When Charlie comes home late to dinner, talking Black ("I was at the li-bary") and when her father taunts her for her "Black" talk and disapproves of her Black friends, we could be watching *West Side Story.* In true rebellion (against parents) for rebellion's sake, when Sam, the documentary maker, asks what her parents think about her style of dress and her speech, Raven says, "They hate it. But their parents hated what they did." Sam asks, "So it's about rebelling against your parents?" Raven responds, "It's about doing what the fuck you wanna do."

Interracial Dating

Another major issue in a hip-hop America is interracial dating. The fear of white girls and Black boys partnering may be as close to the heart of contemporary mainstream criticism of hip-hop as it was to D. W. Griffith. Griffith and his *Birth of a*

Nation–era cronies argued that ending slavery and accepting integration was tantamount to inviting wild, unrestrained sex between Black men and white women. *Malibu's Most Wanted* flips the script on the old racial politics' tendency to define interracial relationships as a Black male/white female thing. On the contrary, it explores the idea of the white guy down with hip-hop whose object of desire is a Black girl. Shondra (Regina Hall) is the bait used to lure B-Rad into the "scared white" expedition. She stands in stark contrast to the blond-haired, blue-eyed prototype of Euro-American beauty. Ironically, Bo Derek, a 1970s blond-haired, blue-eyed icon, is cast as B-Rad's mom (Beth), reinforcing a shifting measuring rod for American beauty even for white youth, in part ushered in by hip-hop.

In this world, Shondra and women who look like her are the new standard. B-Rad lets us know it: "I ain't never been with a real Black girl before—except on the Internet. You the finest girl I been with in my life." Shondra remains the object of men's affection throughout the film. She's the ultimate prize, the trophy. Even when B-Rad veers off course, his distraction doesn't come in a blond-haired, blue-eyed package, but rather as several Black women with whom he ends up in bed. By the movie's end, he wins Shondra over. The film closes with the two of them together fulfilling their dreams: Shondra finally opens her own salon and B-Rad is finally secure with his identity. He reminds Shondra that she was the only one who "appreciated me for who I am."

In the multicultural hip-hop world, Black women are beautiful too. This isn't a new revelation, but *Malibu's Most Wanted* takes the issue head-on. The fact that white men have historically admired Black women receives little public attention.* In a similar vein, in place of the Ku Klux Klan–style mob justice that has been one of the most visible historical responses to the fear of Black men dating white women, *Malibu's Most Wanted* gives us Tek, the Black man upset because he fears his baby momma (Shondra) is dating a white guy. Much of the plot in the last third of the film is driven by Tek's desire to find out if Shondra is dating B-Rad and if so, to put a stop to it. This *Birth of a Nation* parody is one of several moments when the film reveals its intention to confront the old racial politics.

In *Bulworth* and *Bringing Down the House* interracial dating is trumped by the traditional older man/younger woman scenario, specifically, older white men who fall for young Black women. In *Black and White*, interracial dating is steeped in the old racial politics. Rather than examine the complexities of interracial relationships, the film is so focused on interracial sex—and sex alone—that the human interaction between Blacks and whites never materializes. Although Will's tryst with two Black women is an exception, all the other interracial relationships are between Black men and white women. White women and Black men do in fact date, so this isn't totally outlandish. Yet the treatment in *Black and White*, whether it involves Will and the two nameless, faceless Black girls or Greta

---

*Even Halle Berry's roles alongside white men in *Swordfish*, *Rich Man's Wife*, *Monster's Ball* and *Die Another Day* are reduced to sex. There is no in-depth exploration of interracial dating. Berry's character is reduced to either a sexpot, a white woman substitute or both.

and Dean, or Greta and Rich, or Rich and Charlie or Rich and Raven, the scenario is the same: a simplistic focus on sex. At one point in the film Rich says to Raven, "I kind of think of you and Charlie as a team." There is no love or even friendship— just lust. This point is driven home in the opening scene where Rich (who is Black), Charlie and Raven (who are white), have sex in the middle of the day in Central Park.

"What is happening in no small part is because of hip-hop," Toback explains. "There's been a breakdown in the restrictions in all behavior, including sexual behavior. In the last few years, interracial sex is natural, casual, normal. Hip-hop if it never does anything else will have achieved that." Ironically, what Toback envisions is the anti-hip-hop crusaders' greatest fear. Again, this simplistic, outdated approach to interracial dating limits the range and hence the impact of this film.

Films that fall short of their promise (e.g., *Black and White*) and those that go the distance (e.g., *Malibu's Most Wanted*) both reveal that America's old racial politics is still with us, even as we try to construct a new language and theoretical framework for engaging race. Films that explore the place where white kids meet hip-hop do for audiences what hip-hop has done for white hip-hop kids: reveal hip-hop as a vehicle to educate and bring down the walls of ignorance when it comes to American race relations.

The old racial politics insists that the multicultural hip-hop space is simply white kids appropriating Black youth culture. Advocates on both sides of the racial divide, operating out of the worldview of the old racial politics, maintain that a racist culture must and will, without fail, be handed down from one generation to the next. While these films dabble in that terrain, they also take us far beyond it to reveal the ways Martin Luther King Jr.'s dream and the American promise of a cultural melting pot is being further actualized by the younger generation. But in this world of America's new racial politics there is another constant: there are no fixed rules. Everything is subject to investigation, interrogation and overthrow. The film *8 Mile* reveals this, as we'll see when we turn to a discussion of the white rapper Eminem, the self-described hip-hop Elvis who's been dubbed the king of hip-hop.

5

Fear of a Culture Bandit

Eminem, the Source *and America's Racial Politics (Old and New)*

Race plays a part in almost everything in America.
—Johnnie Cochran, *Savoy* (October 2003)

In the fall of 2003, the owners of *The Source* magazine held a press conference at a Manhattan hotel. The press conference involved a listening session of a top-selling artist's unreleased material, an unusual move for a magazine, even one exclusively devoted to hip-hop. Rather than a celebration of the rapper's work, however, the session was part of *The Source*'s yearlong campaign to derail the career of the tremendously famous and extremely successful white rapper Eminem. On this wintry late-autumn night in New York City, *Source* owner Dave Mays and the enigmatic rapper Ray Benzino charged that Eminem was a closet racist who hates Black women. To prove it, they unveiled an Eminem recording denigrating Black women with sexist lyrics, referring to them as "niggas" and describing their supposed inferiority to white women.

"Girls I like have big butts/no they don't, 'cause I don't like that nigga shit. . . Blacks and whites they sometimes mix/But Black girls only want your money/cause they be dumb chicks."

From the outset *The Source* anti-Eminem crusade, which began long before these lyrics were unearthed, was largely marked by a racialist perspective. Eminem shouldn't be the recipient of the rap community's largess, they argued, because he's white. And since hip-hop is primarily a Black youth sub-culture, Black rappers rather than white ones should enjoy the spoils. *The Source* owners further claimed that hip-hop was losing its soul, that the essence of the culture was under attack and that hip-hop risked going the way of rock and roll. Eminem, Mays and Benzino declared in countless media interviews over the course of the year, was on the fast track to becoming hip-hop's Elvis, a thinly veiled reference to the process by which Elvis came to be more closely identified with rock and roll, a Black American creation, than Black Americans themselves.

Although *The Source*'s Eminem monomania hinted at several other agendas (more about that later), a close look at this very public mud slinging demonstrates that what was really happening was not so much in the tradition of battle rapping—a hip-hop rite of verbal jostling between two opposing emcees—but was a collision between America's old and new racial politics.

The old racial politics rooted deep in the annals of America's unreconciled racial history relies heavily on stereotypical assumptions about race and exclusivity. Much of the race card–heavy criticism levied against Eminem by the *Source* followed that tradition to the letter. By contrast, a new racial politics has emerged with this generation that makes it more difficult for the old arguments to stick. This new racial politics is coming into its own with a younger generation socialized around the dream of an inclusive America. It's enhanced by a youth popular culture, hip-hop, which prides itself on mass cross-cultural appeal, and it insists that the old racial politics is too limited for engaging or defining America today. The old definitions no longer universally apply. Eminem advances that new perspective in some of his lyrics, but he also does a lot more.

Born Marshall Mathers in Joseph, Kansas, in 1972, Eminem spent his formative years in Detroit in the working-class 8 Mile neighborhood. He dropped out of high school after repeating the ninth grade for the third time, held a series of unfulfilling service industry jobs and married his high school sweetheart when he was twenty-six years old. His life story is an open book. A suicide attempt, estranged relationships with his wife and mother and a missing father are all recurring subjects in his lyrics. He openly admits in interviews that his father was never around and his mom was an inadequate parent. (His dad conveniently reappeared upon his son's newfound fame and his mom later sued him for defamation and settled out of court.)

Although he began rapping at 14, over the next decade he enjoyed only moderate local recognition with a few singles and one solo album project, *Infinite*, in 1996, both on independent labels (not unusual for aspiring rappers post-1995). His career as a rapper didn't blossom until 1997, when he competed in a Rap Olympics emcee battle in Los Angeles and shortly afterward caught the eye of Jimmy Iovine, part-owner of Interscope Records, the same Interscope that helped launch Death Row Records in 1992. Iovine linked Eminem up with Dr. Dre, the legendary rapper/producer of NWA and Death Row fame, and the result was Eminem's first major album, *Slim Shady*, which was produced by Dr. Dre and released by Interscope in February 1999. The album debuted at number 2 and sold 300,000 units in its first week.

In 2000 came Eminem's second major CD, entitled *Marshall Mathers* (which sold 1.7 million copies in its first week and over 8 million units in two months), followed by a third, *The Eminem Show*, in 2002, which sold over 1.3 million copies its first week and over 7.6 million by the end of 2002 (both produced by Dr. Dre). From his debut on the national stage in 1999 up to the 2003 release of his film *8 Mile*, Eminem was routinely vilified for his antifamily values, antigay, antigovernment and antiauthority rebel-without-a-cause lyrics. The content of his first two major label releases vacillates between Jerry Springer–like family drama, more metaphors than you can shake a stick at and typical teen rebelliousness. By the time *The Eminem Show* was released, he began focusing more on the type of youth alienation specific to those coming of age in the 1980s and 1990s global economy, accompanied by its schizophrenic racial politics (old and new warring together), complete with anti-woman "bitch and ho talk" commonplace in mainstream 1990s chart-topping hip-hop. His was an in-your-face confrontational rap style rooted in his freestyle battle rap beginnings which—when spiced up with a Marilyn-Manson-meets-hip-hop approach, cut with a Michael Myers-esque tongue-in-cheek sense of comedy and several run-ins with the law (in 2000 for assault and gun possession)—made evergreen the idea that Eminem equals controversy.

His personal story of holding a series of odd jobs in the service industry while trying to make his way as a rapper, which became the narrative thrust for the film *8 Mile*, isn't vastly different from countless other aspiring rappers. Where his story differs is in his skin color, a chance meeting with Dr. Dre and Iovine and an eagerness on their part (with Eminem's cooperation at the very least) to cash in on Em's whiteness.

Central to the argument posed by Mays and Benzino are the same issues that have hampered even the most in-depth analysis of Eminem: the question of his talent relative to Black rappers, the notion that he's the Elvis of hip-hop and the possibility that he's stealing record sales from Black rappers. The problem here is not simply that Eminem is white and can rap—but that he's white, can rap so well, has received honor after honor as a rap great by the entertainment establishment (two Grammys for *Slim Shady* and three for *Marshall Mathers*) and that for thirty years hip-hop has been almost exclusively associated with Black Americans. The contrast is so striking it begs a reaction, especially in an America where the old racial politics still dictates what's acceptable. In such a climate a white rapper, no matter how good, is bound to be considered suspect by Blacks. It is not unprecedented in America's white supremacist culture for mediocre whites who perform as well as Blacks, in an area dominated by Blacks, to find themselves elevated through the stratosphere (European ballplayers in the NBA, for example).

By the fall of 2003, Eminem's whiteness was fast proving to be a cash cow. After the release of *The Eminem Show* in 2002 and on the eve of the release of *8 Mile,* almost overnight he was transformed from a foul-mouthed white rapper novelty spewing antifamily values into a cultural icon—with a box office–busting film grossing $54 million opening weekend, a best-selling soundtrack (700,000 in the first week) and endless magazine covers, including the *New York Times Magazine, People, Vibe* and *Entertainment Weekly*. Such was the euphoria of the new converts, especially the baby boomers, that his performance in the film *8 Mile* even generated a brief Oscar buzz. In 2002 alone, he reportedly earned $27 million (according to *Rolling Stone,* April 3, 2003) and, along with other new projects, secured producing credit for the soundtrack for the film *Resurrection,* which chronicled the life of the late rap great Tupac Shakur. Even before the release of his CD *Encore* in November 2004, he'd sold more than 50 million CDs collectively since 1999.

The success of a white boy in a Black-dominated medium in a predominantly white society, more than anything else, is a crash course in America's racial politics. On the one hand, given his upbringing as an outcast outsider in a nation that feeds on its young and in an economy with narrowing options for working-class youth, he's a victim, oppressed. On the other hand, in a society where the caste system of whiteness often prevails and still bestows privilege, he's part of the oppressor class. But it's the latter identification that Em's *Source* critics have focused on.

Contradictions and Conflicts

These are the dynamics involved when a magazine with Black content but significant white ownership charges racism. Given Eminem's killer instinct for cutting through the old racial politics, he naturally shot back. Now 31, he issued a public apology, explaining that he made the recording when he was a naive sixteen-year-old: "Ray Benzino, Dave Mays and *The Source* have had a vendetta against me, Shady Records and our artists for a long time," he said, referring to the treatment he had received from *The Source* over the years, as well as more recently his protégé 50 Cent. "The tape they played today was something I made out of anger, stupidity and frustration when I was a teenager. I'd just broken up with my girlfriend, who was African American, and I reacted like the angry, stupid kid I was. I hope people will take it for the foolishness that it was, not for what somebody is trying to make it into today."

Several days later Russell Simmons's Hip-Hop Summit Action Network issued a statement in support of Eminem:

These lyrics are disgusting, but the oneness of hip-hop culture has transformed many young people in trailer parks around the country away from their parents' old mindset of white supremacy. We believe Eminem's apology is sincere and forthright. He continues not only to be an icon of hip-hop, but also has evolved into a good soldier who gives back money, time and energy to the community, encouraging this generation of youth to reach their highest aspirations.

Dave Mays resigned from the board of the Network in protest.

Several months later, *The Source* released a free CD of the lyrics in question with its February 2004 issue, which Eminem unsuccessfully attempted to block in court. The battle raged on or fizzled, depending on which pundits you read. Eminem shot back with another press release. A series of dis records back and forth between Benzino and Eminem followed, with similar recurring themes. At one point Benzino likened himself to Malcolm X and referred to Eminem as the Hitler of rap.

The allegation that Eminem is a racist and hates Black women, as *Source* owners put it, must be situated in the context of the magazine's ongoing beef with Eminem.

"Don't make this right now a double standard," Benzino said at the press conference. "We gotta treat this the same way you treat Mike Tyson, like you treat Kobe Bryant, like you treat R. Kelly, like you treat O.J. Simpson."

Of course Ray Benzino has his own personal interest at stake, making his charge suspect. Take a walk in his shoes. After a decade in the game rife with mediocre sales, he sees a white rapper get mad love and be hailed as the best ever. This has got to be a hard pill to swallow, especially in a Black-dominated musical format, expecially when your manager owns the most influential magazine in the business. Over the years, Mays has assisted Benzino's rap interests a great deal—managing Benzino's career, providing him coverage and ad space in the magazine and maintaining an open affiliation with Benzino, which certainly didn't hurt Benzino in his ability to secure big-name guest appearances on his albums. Still, by the summer of 2003, according to the *Los Angeles Times,* Benzino had not sold more than 250,000 units collectively in over a decade of various album releases under various names. Without a doubt the ghosts of *The Source* staff walkout in 1994 continue to haunt him.* It's likely something that Benzino may never recover from. Unlike the followers of self-appointed Black American leaders, hip-hop fans, if Benzino's experience is any indication, are unforgiving. He's enjoyed a few hit singles, has gotten access to the best producers and collabos, but his attempt to cash in on an emcee battle with Eminem, even in a climate where emcee battles proved lucrative, was too enormous a leap of faith.

Never far from the battlefront was the not-so-distant time when *The Source* had celebrated Eminem in its "Unsigned Hype" column in 1998, shortly before his national acclaim. Subsequent feature stories in the magazine followed his historic rise. But somewhere along the line the relationship soured. Selwyn Hinds, the former editor in chief of *Source* who had a hand in Eminem's first coverage in the magazine, offers some

---

*The 1994 *Source* editorial staff walkout is legendary in hip-hop circles. See Jeff Chang, *Can't Stop, Won't Stop* (2005), for a detailed recap of the chain of events that led to the editorial staff upheaval. In brief, the editorial staff, by its account, quit in response to a move by publisher Dave Mays to secure coverage for Benzino in *The Source.* Both sides were a bit overzealous in their attempt to have things their way, ultimately avoiding a middle ground. For whatever reasons, the editors refused Benzino coverage and Mays took the position that Benzino was unfairly singled out.

insight into the early head butting between Dave Mays and Eminem in a brilliant essay, "Young Black Teenagers," one of the most important pieces yet written about white kids and hip-hop, in his *Gunshots in My Cook-up: Bits and Bites of a Caribbean Hip-Hop Life* (2003).

If Eminem is exhibit one of the white presence in hip-hop, my old boss Dave Mays, owner and publisher of *The Source* magazine is exhibit two. Mays was a walking, breathing avatar of the general, surface perception of hip-hop. The clothes, the jewelry, the cars. You name it; he rocked it . . . He'd been down with hip-hop for a long time, a part and parcel of its fabric since high school in the eighties all the way through his college days at Harvard, where he started *The Source* as a newsletter. You couldn't question his sincerity and commitment lightly. Mays loved hip-hop; especially it's hardcore, rougher elements. And oh, did he look upon other white folk with deep suspicion. Mays would be quick to snort with scorn about "these white boys running around like they hip-hop," a comment that could encompass anyone, from writers, to fans, to music industry executives. His self-indoctrination in hip-hop's street ethos would, upon occasion, even cause him to cast that suspicious eye beyond white folk, nudging me to inquire if so-and-so writer wasn't perhaps, a bit too "bourgie" to really understand hardcore hip-hop. That so-and-so editor was just too damn "corny" and altogether out of touch with hip-hop . . . I never understood the ease with which he could say and think such things about young black journalists who clearly were attuned to hip-hop . . . Yet they didn't register high enough on his personal meter. It demonstrated a remarkable sense of authority and presumption, not to mention a class-oriented bias that seemed ludicrous coming from a Harvard-educated white kid. Then a year later a very smart, young white writer I later worked with put it in context. Jon Caramanica—also a Harvard-educated hip-hop head, ironically enough—and I were sitting in the offices of 360hiphop.com the day after I attended the Wu-Tang show at the Hammerstein Ballroom, musing about the all-white hip-hop crowd and the attitudes of some white boys in hip-hop. Jon might have been talking about the kids at the show, but he made me understand Mays and his ilk better.

"Look," he said, "it's like a sliding scale. As a white boy in hip-hop, you gotta have someone on the scale below you. First, it's all the corny white kids, then the ones new to hip-hop. The ones trying really hard. Clearly you're cooler than that. But then you start measuring yourself up to the black kids, thinking surely you're cooler, more hip-hop than the ones who don't seem to wear hip-hop on their sleeve, the ones who you perceive as corny. Then you start thinking you're more hip-hop than they are."

Selwyn's assessment of David Mays brings to mind the Edgar Allen Poe short story "William Wilson." It's the tale of a schoolboy who's the cat's meow. No one's smarter than him. No one's faster than him. None of his peers can compete on any level with him. He's the best at everything from the playground to the chalkboard. Then comes along a new boy at school. He's just as good as William—at everything. William's greatest fear is that he just might be better. He's even got the same name, William. William Wilson has met someone nearly identical to him and it drives him mad.

Like William Wilson, Mays has far too long enjoyed his status as the Blackest white boy on the block. Then along comes Eminem. Not only is he down with Blacks and hip-hop but he can rap too—as well as many Black rappers. When Wilson is stunned, his response is to kill William. Is Mays's response to Eminem character assassination?

Neither Mays nor Benzino has a long history of political engagement or concern. And as owners of a magazine whose content is hip-hop, they're engaging in exactly the same business practice as Eminem. *The Source* never stopped to see the irony in this, whether attacking Eminem, or 50 Cent and Dr. Dre for being guilty by association. Mays and Benzino also missed the irony that *The Source,* which has always been at least partially white-owned, was carrying out the very same act at the core of their supposed ire. Neither did the thought arise during the magazine's fifteen-year history that the music industry (most certainly the major record labels) was exploiting hip-hop to a tune that Eminem could never imagine. Ripping off countless artists. Taking the lion's share and then some. But *The Source* never came to *their* defense, having benefited from a symbiotic relationship with the music industry via advertising in the magazine and hip-hop industry insiders that provided endless fodder for *Source* covers, feature stories, awards shows, Web site content and more.* These contradictions mysteriously escaped their politically correct radar.

In their defense, perhaps Mays and Benzino fall into the "forced radicals" category that Alain Locke, the Harlem Renaissance writer, identified in the *New Negro* more than a half century ago at a point when white influence over Black art was as significant as it is today in the era of hip-hop.

> Of course, the thinking Negro has shifted a little toward the left with the world-trend, and there is an increasing group who affiliate with radical and liberal movements. But fundamentally for the present the Negro is radical on race matters, conservative on others, in other words, a "forced radical," a social protestant rather than a genuine radical. Yet under further pressure and injustice iconoclastic thought and motives will inevitably increase.

Like Eminem, Mays refrains from using the n-word and derides whites who are racist, but until now has kept a pretty low profile when it comes to race matters. The possibility that Em could be the Elvis of hip-hop could be Mays's radicalizing

---

*Although many *Source* haters claim that the *Source* editorial pages are for sale, this is something that has never been substantiated by this author and seems more conspiracy theory coming from anticommercial hip-hop crusaders than an idea rooted in fact.

event. A fierce advocate of hip-hop, Mays has not only built a business around it but his very life. An Eminem turned Elvis shakes the very foundation of his identity.

Alain Locke's comments were directed at Black Americans. His landscape ironically involved similar dynamics—a period of great African American productivity and art controlled by white elite money. Shortly after the Harlem Renaissance, during the rise of the American film industry, African Americans were again exploited by white elites. Hollywood in its golden age would become central in the American imagination and confine African Americans to roles that would be devastating for generations to come. This historic moment is echoed in the debate over Eminem and the white engagement with hip-hop.

"It's hard to argue what an individual is feeling, but an argument can be made about young white hip-hop kids putting on a guise," Melvin Donaldson, author of *Black Directors in Hollywood* (2003), told me when I recently asked him about the similarities between Hollywood's golden age and today's hip-hop as a site of Black exploitation. Donaldson continues:

> With blackface you can take it off. White hip-hop kids can turn their caps around, put a belt in their pants and go to the mall without being followed. Black people have to deal with oppression, but also character types that the hip-hop industry has created with the music by continuing the thug and gangsta stereotypes about Blacks. White hip-hop kids can pick and choose without repercussions and the full weight of racial stereotypes.

As a young college-educated white coming of age in the Northeast, deeply immersed in Black youth culture in the 1980s and 1990s, the Harlem Renaissance, Hollywood's golden age and the more recent Afrocentric era that raised the question of Black exploitation in the entertainment industry, Mays could hardly miss the implication of hip-hop as a site of exploitation. Given the magazine's track record—avoiding liquor and cigarette advertising, for example—Black exploitation is something Mays consciously guards against. But in a world where the old racial politics is spun on its head, even when we veer eerily close, exploitation doesn't always neatly fit old formulas. African American record executives, from Russell Simmons to P. Diddy to Suge Knight, have unashamedly had as significant a hand in peddling stereotypical images of Black Americans as their white counterparts, even as the major labels hold the most influential cards. White exploitation of Blacks in entertainment is historic. Black collusion has been taken to a whole new level in the hip-hop era. So whether, say, Dr. Dre is in Ruthless Records, Death Row or Aftermath clothing doesn't sway the final outcome. He's still advancing images of Blacks that reinforce stereotypes at the same time as they reveal an emerging new Black youth culture.

Which brings us back to Eminem.

A Black Thing? and Other Hip-Hop Truths

The charges that Mays and Benzino make against Eminem ignore critical aspects of the emerging politics of race. A few details about hip-hop, of which *The Source* owners and most other hip-hop aficionados are well aware, should place this alleged emcee battle squarely in middle of the cross fire between old and new racial politics.

To begin with, it must be stated unequivocally that hip-hop is a subculture of Black American youth culture—period. Yes, it's become en vogue to imagine hip-hop as belonging to everyone. Sure, there have been other cultural influences. But influences are just that, influences. Black American cultural attitudes, style, verbal and body language, as well as insider Black cultural perspective, not only were prevalent at hip-hop's origins but remain at its core today. There is room for an argument to be made of a greater melting pot when it comes to hip-hop culture's origins in the less commercialized elements of graffiti and perhaps break dancing. But when it comes to the verbal art of rapping and the accompanying body language and images that are being bought and sold in our age of global commerce, Black American culture is the primary culture in hip-hop. This is why Eminem is such a striking figure. Even at a time when hip-hop has entered the mainstream, a white rapper with the skill, style and attitude of Eminem is a rarity in a sea of Black rappers who, by contrast, aren't operating so far beyond their own culture.

Yet statements like the ones made by *Spin* associate editor Dave Itzkoff, when he was interviewed for a story on the Eminem/Benzino conflict (*Daily News*, January 22, 2003), reflect the growing opinion that, when speaking of hip-hop today, Blackness is coincidental and increasingly irrelevant. "It's a slippery slope when you make the argument that hip-hop is only a black person's art," Itzkoff said. "Certainly its origins are in that community, but if you want it to endure as an art form, you have to let other people have their way with it." Itzkoff is not alone. Legions of new converts are eager to embrace hip-hop now that it has embedded itself in mainstream popular culture. And they have convinced themselves that the influences matter more and the Black cultural origins matter less—to the extent that it's more common to elevate hip-hop as an everyone thing than to talk about it as a Black thing.*

At a conference organized around the theme, "Hip-Hop and Social Change," held at Chicago's Field Museum of Natural History in the fall of 2003, this question of origins sparked a fierce debate during the question-and-answer segment of a panel discussion. One panelist took the position that hip-hop isn't a Black thing. This elicited a few heated statements from folks in the audience. One young man got into a back-and-forth exchange with the panelist in question, who was of South American descent, after she used her age and backnthaday Rock Steady Crew affiliation to pull rank. "The argument that hip-hop is not a Black thing actually weakens hip-hop," says Marcyliena Morgan, director of the Hiphop Archive at Stanford University. "Everyone wants to say they love hip-hop

---

*I use the term "Black" in reference to hip-hop's origins as elsewhere to indicate people of African descent, whether they hail from Africa or the African diaspora. The term "Black" rather than "African American," as poet Haki Madhubuti observed in his *Black Men: Obsolete, Single, Dangerous? The Afrikan American Family in Transition* (1990), is the more inclusive term. My point is to avoid the distinctions of African American and Caribbean American (including Puerto Rican and Dominican American) and yield to the more unifying term, not to discredit contributions to hip-hop and influences from various racial and ethnic backgrounds.

now. It's okay to love it. But to say you love it is to say you love Black things. People need to interrogate why they don't want to say that they love Blackness."

Dr. Morgan, author of *The Real Hip-Hop: Battling for Knowledge, Power and Respect in the Underground* (Dulce University Press, 2005), believes it's up to scholars to make it clear how and why hip-hop came out of the African American experience. "All the aspects of hip-hop are implanted in the genetic code of the African American experience. It was that experience which provided the space for hip-hop to emerge. Life is not life without movement, without music. That music is something you bring into your homes, your schools, into your streets and all around you. There are all these examples of African Americans turning the street, the subway station, etc., into the concert hall. Hip-hop is the urban experience of embracing music in these ways. The experience of dancing in the street is not new. The defiance and the politics associated with that is new. Hip-hop is the symbol for people internationally for how you need to organize based on the reality that we've done it and are struggling in the belly of the beast. That is why during the Ukrainian election they made a hip-hop song and everybody used it."

Of course many young Blacks in the hip-hop industry also take the position that hip-hop is not a Black thing. They too, as Dr. Morgan says, "need to interrogate why they don't say they love Blackness." Many of them haven't developed a concrete political perspective that helps them jibe the new racial politics with the old. They may have tons of political opinions, but opinions do not a political perspective make. It's easier for them to view hip-hop as a universal artistic space or as a strictly musical phenomenon than it is for them to tease out the intricacies of their own politics or confront the demons of their own contradictions—contradictions that we all share and that are part and parcel of a contemporary America haunted by unresolved issues of race.

A second hip-hop truth is that hip-hop prides itself on its multicultural appeal. When it comes to hip-hop, skill comes first. That Eminem was embraced by Black hip-hop kids is in large part what allowed for Eminem's rise up the ranks, not some one-dimensional conspiracy of whiteness. Some critics charge that white media folk and other gatekeepers gave Eminem greater access at an earlier stage in his career than Black hip-hop artists have been afforded. This criticism implies a conspiracy of whiteness. More than a conspiracy, a rarely discussed variable is the large number of young whites who love hip-hop, work in the hip-hop industry and are anxious to see one of their own compete on the same level with Black rappers. It is no secret or surprise that many were excited about Eminem.

That said, there are also those working in media outside of the industry who wield influence and frantically await the great white hope—be he a boxer, a European NBA star or a rapper. Likewise among those not to be overlooked are baby boomers, again outside the industry, seeking to understand their children's fascination with hip-hop. They can't stomach an Ol' Dirty Bastard or relate to a DMX, but they will at least hear Eminem out. This white x-factor is also a testament to the fact that Blacks don't run the business of hip-hop, a much more substantial argument to make for those who really want to delve into the arena of protest politics.

America in the early 2000s is not America of the 1960s, 1970s or even 1980s. How race is lived in America has shifted. But the charges of racism leveled against Eminem don't allow for that shifting reality. Eminem is white, yes, but he comes from a working-class background. This fact, and what it means to be white and working class in today's America, can never be minimized. Eminem comes from a socioeconomic background not vastly different from that of many Black rappers. Like his Black counterparts, he's a victim of American's education and economic policies of the 1980s and 1990s—from inadequate schooling and education budget cuts to NAFTA. People like Eminem are realizing that dysfunctional schools are a track to a future of mediocrity. Rather than fall into the trap, they are dropping out of school. Either way, the jobs available for working-class youth are dismal. This is something that has affected Black American youth in general and increasingly white youth too, including aspiring rappers, including Eminem. This new reality does not totally dismiss the persistence of white skin privilege, but the charges of the white rapper getting over on the back of Black pain and suffering isn't the actual picture in this case.

A third hip-hop truth is that artists rap about what they know, generally their own life experiences—the more true to life, the better in the eyes of fans.* This truth was etched in

---

*In the early to mid-1980s many hip-hop artists who secured record deals came out of middle-class backgrounds. Some even were college educated. This shifted dramatically by the 1990s, when many of the big-name rap stars to emerge had origins in poor and working-class

stone by the early 1990s. Eminem is not deep in the streets in an era where street culture is essentially defined by the drug game; hustling, pimps, bitches and hos have become the dominant message in commercially driven hip-hop music. Keeping it real, he turns to what he knows and sticks to the formula of misogyny and gunplay far more than die-hard Eminem fans are willing to admit. But not deep in the streets himself, he runs short on material to keep up with the grittiest Black from the projects, East or West Coaster. Hence he turns to his own life for a Jerry Springer–esque real-life drama that struck a nerve with kids for whom the pimps, gangstas and hustlers were far too much "cultural safari" at the end of the day. But it must be noted, particularly for those dying to elevate Eminem above any Black rapper to ever grab a mic, that as an artist who is willing to defy the formula, he's not unique. Countless artists do it every day (scores of local and regional emcees) and don't get national recognition. Some have done it and enjoyed great fame (the Fugees, Lauryn Hill, Kanye West). In that

---

communities. This fact helped give voice to the early 1990s expression "keep it real." Although the trend of rising incarceration began in the mid- to late 1970s, it isn't until the late 1980s that we began to see the lines blur between prison culture and hip-hop culture, given the numbers of young Black men entering and exiting the criminal justice system. So the shifting content of hip-hop lyrics from the mid-1980s era, when the content seemed more diverse, to the 1990s street culture–dominated lyrics and so-called gangsta style was not strictly coincidental. Additionally, the terms "nigga" and "bitch" in reference to young Black men and women in hip-hop didn't gain significant frequency until the early 1990s. This has more to do with prison culture than with class—as has been the charge of Black elites.

regard, Eminem is not as revolutionary a figure as he's been cast relative to the wider world of hip-hop. But he does offer another distinctive voice and style to the field of hip-hop, as other distinctive rappers have done before and since.

Finally on the list of hip-hop truths to consider is the hard, cold fact that hip-hop has been so thoroughly associated with young Blacks and the urban ghetto that it is difficult (though not impossible) to divorce it from Black American youth. In today's age of visual images, racial dynamics have dramatically shifted from what they were in previous eras. Eminem's most outspoken critics raise the alarm of culture banditry, but the possibilities of hip-hop ever duplicating the path taken by rock and roll, or even jazz and blues, must be weighted against hip-hop's visual Black stamp.

Appropriation and the New Racial Politics

Collectively these four truths—hip-hop as a subculture of Black youth culture, hip-hop priding itself on cross-cultural appeal, artists' tendency to rap about real life, and hip-hop's association with young Black men in the popular imagination—reveal that we indeed are living in the age of appropriation. But hip-hop is not the first time Black culture has been appropriated—nor will it be the last. In fact Black culture is being appropriated anew in our lifetime. In a 2003 year-end special issue cover story, while Michael Jackson almost daily was receiving what Supreme Court Justice Clarence Thomas once called a high-tech lynching, *Rolling Stone* magazine dubbed white R&B sensation Justin Timberlake the new king of pop.

In a *New York Times* arts page lead story (November 3, 2002) a year earlier Neil Strauss wrote,

> As surprising as it is, considering the long tradition of white artists riding black musical styles to the top of the charts, there are extremely few white men successfully singing R&B today. But as the distance between hip-hop and R&B narrows and an 80's nostalgia creeps into popular culture, the field is changing.

The story was entitled "Blue-Eyed Rhythm and Blues: Does Race Matter?" and ran alongside a photo of Justin Timberlake from that year's MTV Music Awards show, where he borrowed Michael Jackson's moonwalk act, complete with the hat and glove (two gloves rather than one). At the time, Timberlake had yet to launch his solo career and was still performing with the multiplatinum-selling boy band 'N Sync. Timberlake's first album, *Justified,* produced by the Neptunes and Timberland— both popular with Black hip-hop and R&B stars—would come later. Strauss is correct that few young white men are singing R&B and hip-hop, but this doesn't mean that appropriation of Black youth culture hasn't been extensive in terms of culture and style. The outer packaging is familiar, while the contents inside vary. From Britney, Christina and Mariah to boy bands like 'N Sync to hip-hop/rock bands like Limp Bizkit, Korn and Linkin Park (dubbed rock-rap hybrids), the style and cultural packaging prevails, even when the content is shifting.

What Strauss is getting at may explain why no other white rapper has emerged since Eminem who parallels his visibility and success. If indeed hip-hop is headed the way of rock and roll, the way critics charge, and Em is leading the pack, why then have we not seen other white hip-hop acts break through at the same level? Despite a flurried search for the next great white rapper following Em's success, the hip-hop music industry has been cautious. The idea of a white rapper may be more of a sell as a novelty than as the norm. Perhaps hip-hop has become so strongly identified with young Blacks that it's nearly impossible to separate the two ideas.

Eminem's lyrics alone, when he's commenting on race, are a journey into why white kids love hip-hop. That, along with Dre and Em deciding to team up, explains part of the emerging racial politics. Eminem's analysis of race is the dominant, but least discussed, theme in his lyrics and may prove to be in the final analysis his major impact as a rap artist. Em represents the new racial politics. He understands the knee-jerk reaction of the old racial politics as well and articulates it repeatedly in his lyrics. Yet his critics' attacks come straight out of the playbook of the old racial politics. He gets it; they don't. He points out the old racial politics at work relative to hip-hop on his own CDs: white Americans are afraid that their children are like him; that Dr. Dre, a Black hip-hop legend, helped him rise to the top; that he is benefiting from white race privilege; and that both he and Dre are gaining greater access to each other's audience as a result.

Eminem's critics are quick to hold him accountable for misogynist and anti-Black lyrics, but do not attack Black rappers for the same language. Seemingly, misogyny is acceptable —perhaps expected—when Black rappers are articulating it.

In fact, Black rappers have given white rappers, including Eminem, a green light for such commentary, given the endless diatribes on "bitches" and "hos," generally referring to young Black women. If Eminem is joining the company of hip-hop lyricists, could he really be down if he didn't do the same? Reaction to Eminem suggests that it is not so much his verbal attacks on Black women that are the problem, as it is his attacks on Blacks in general. At the same time, when it comes to race, a double standard is at work. Blacks have been calling each other "nigger" via hip-hop for too long and, truth be told, have let too many whites off the hook for using the n-word as well.

Further, racist commentary is part of the narrative of the old racial politics. It's not surprising at all that Eminem used racial epithets to describe Blacks. When Ice Cube used racist language, describing white women as "cave bitches," and Jew-bashed Jerry Heller for his association with Eazy-E, he too was a teenager. Today he enjoys careers in both film and rap, and his critics have almost universally allowed him to leave his racist diatribes in the sandlot of his teenage years. Why should Eminem be held to a higher moral standard? We of the hip-hop generation who try to bring forth a new racial politics are not free of the old. Eminem, like all of us, is a product of America's unresolved race relations. As such, who among us has never used a racial slur, if not in public then at least under our breath? Unlike most of us, Eminem just finds himself in the uncanny position of having his racist laundry part of the public record.

Eminem's success exposes at least two things. First that this post–baby boom generation of young whites is an age-group whose racial lens is unprecedented. It is not perfect, it is not without fissures, it is not free of bias, but it's nonetheless unprecedented. And second, many baby boomers see Eminem as their only access to the world of hip-hop that their children are embracing. Without him, they'd be clueless. For these parents, Eminem, even with his blemishes, is the savior of lost white kids that they'd been praying for.

"It's kind of strange," Eminem told the *New York Times Magazine* about his expanding concert audience in a cover story entitled "Mr. Ambassador." "It used to range from 10 years old to 25. Now it seems to be from 5 years old to 55."

Long before mainstream America dubbed Eminem its ambassador to the world of hip-hop, he'd gained acceptance from the hip-hop community itself, where skill takes precedence over skin color. His ghetto pass was his authenticity and his mastery of the art form. Not even Black kids ever unanimously approved his lyrical content (you'd be hard-pressed, for example, to find a Black rapper—even amid the billions of derogatory references to women—who'd ever let a bad word slip from his lips about his momma). But content has always been secondary to flow.

White hip-hop kids also accepted Eminem long before their baby boomer parents did. Some were along for the antiauthority teen rebelliousness ride. Some identified with his vision of America's dysfunctional families. Others who were deeper into the culture, like their Black, Latino, Asian and Native American counterparts, recognized in Eminem's lyrics an alienation similar to what Black rappers articulate—and which really brought hip-hop to the center of youth popular culture.

For years many Black baby boomers have been telling us hip-hop generationers to beware the culture bandit, the white kid who deftly crosses over the preconceived racial divide in style, form and sound. As long as we didn't own the labels and distribution outlets, hip-hop culture, they said—even as we stared at them incredulously—would one day be appropriated in the tradition of rock and roll, which began as anything but white and ended being identified with Elvis Presley.

Amid the Eminem mainstream craze, some younger Blacks also fear that the pain and despair of young Black America (relative to issues like unemployment, education and center-city economic development), which is at the core of hip-hop's message, will be ignored—again—as the spotlight shines instead on a similar but slightly different white middle-class American alienation.

"I'm sick of seeing him being interviewed and him being named the king of rap," Lois Swaysland, a senior at Cleveland State University who lead a boycott of the film *8 Mile*, told me not long before *The Source* anti-Eminem crusade began. "I think it's an insult to African Americans because after music was taken out of our schools we put effort into creating this music with our hands, mouths, et cetera. And then over twenty-five years later along comes this white guy to have his life made into a movie. It reminds me of Elvis all over again."

Swaysland's sentiment echoes the accurate elements of Benzino's and Mays's beef with Eminem. At the same time it mirrors aspects of the old racial politics that die hard.

Nicole Balin, 30, a publicist for hip-hop groups at the Los Angeles–based Ballin' Entertainment. She's been into hip-hop since high school and has worked in various capacities in the hip-hop industry throughout her professional career. I asked Nicole, who's white, if she thought white hip-hop kids shared this fear of the culture bandit. She told me if they did, I'd be hard-pressed to find anyone who would admit it.

"White hip-hop kids have tried so hard to fit into hip-hop culture that to admit that is to admit that we would never be able to culturally mix—it goes against our whole belief system."

Perhaps this is the dilemma of the culture bandit this time around: the naïveté of young Blacks and young whites who dare believe that through hip-hop we could move closer to re-alizing the society that our parents told us we were supposed to be building. The irony is that a new generation of Ameri-cans, Eminem included, have against their best intentions be-come victims of America's old racial politics.

Exploring these dynamics tells us a lot about where we are, where we're headed and how hip-hop reinforces stereotypes about race with one hand, even as it equips us to upend old racial paradigms with the other. America's racial politics is shifting, even as the shift is being resisted. The Eminem phe-nomenon makes clear that as a generation we're beginning to raise the right questions about race in America. The cutting edge of this new racial politics is even more transparent among those seeking to access hip-hop as an agent of social change. It is there that white, Black, Asian and Latino youth are forming alliances and coalitions crucial to the future of the republic.

6

Coalition Building Across Race
Organizing the Hip-Hop Voting Bloc

The cool thing about this political movement is whether the music changes or not, it's really bringing attention to substance in an arena where we haven't had any since the days of Chuck D and X-Clan. It's bringing a sense of "this is my country and I want to do something to change it." The downside of that is that we have a bunch of people that are pushing a movement forward and some of the people we're following may be false gods leading us down a road to their own self gain. Until more people step up and question who's leading them, you're gonna have people in positions where they can gain. But honestly it's a small price to pay to make change in this world.
—Wendy Day, founder, The Rap Coalition

On the whole, the 2004 Democratic National Convention would have come and gone; a lackluster affair—if not for the electrifying speech made by a young state senator from

Illinois. The twenty-minute keynote address by 42-year-old Barack Obama was packed with more substance and bore a greater sense of urgency than speeches delivered by presidential candidate John Kerry and his running mate, John Edwards, combined. But the irony doesn't stop there. Obama is the child of an African immigrant and the product of an interracial marriage, a small detail that means a lot given America's racial politics. Personal circumstances aside, he dared to achieve the impossible on another front: Barack Obama was on the verge of becoming the first Black senator in the United States since Illinois elected Carol Mosley Braun in 1992.

What does any of this have to do with white kids and hip-hop? Consider an overlooked chapter of American political history. Not since Douglas Wilder served as governor of Virginia (1990–1994) over a decade ago, has there been a Black governor—and he was the only Black governor ever elected by the popular vote to head a state in the Union. There have been only two Black U.S. senators since Reconstruction. Only one of these was elected in the last decade, Carol Mosley Braun, the first Black woman senator. Edward Brooke was elected by the people of Massachusetts in 1966 and served two terms (1967–1979). Currently there are no Black governors. This brief history of Black senators and governors is a sad commentary on our democracy. And at a time when America continues to demand democratic governance around the globe, the extent to which the nation has achieved a pluralistic society at home is deplorable. Very little in the electoral arena over the past decade suggests that this can change. Even established Black career politicians who seem likely to be in the running for statewide posts have concluded that they themselves are unelectable in races where they don't have majority Black and Latino voters.

The subtext of conversations about electibility of Blacks, Latinos, Native Americans and Asians—whether silent or spoken—usually focuses on disingenuous ideas like "transcending race," an assumption steeped in outdated racial politics that candidates who aren't white must demonstrate that their first allegiance is to the white majority rather than to any racial, ethnic or cultural group, especially their own. The other old racial politics assumption is that the nonwhite candidate is by definition less qualified. Be that as it may, this conversation never penetrates the subsurface where the more crucial questions of the day regarding race and American politics abound. One of the only arenas where such a discussion is already under way is the arena loosely described as hip-hop politics. Hip-hop politics is arguably one of the few political spaces to have emerged in the past three decades where any real potential exists for challenging prevailing public policy approaches to issues like education, criminal justice, employment, health care and foreign policy.

During the most recent election cycle, much was made of a hip-hop voting bloc. Yet that voting bloc, for the most part, remains undefined. In my 2002 publication (*The Hip-Hop Generation,* 2002), I defined the "hip-hop generation" as African Americans born after the civil rights movement between 1965 and 1984. I also discussed the possibility for young African Americans to create a voting bloc—given the influential Black youth culture and its subculture hip-hop. On further reflection, for hip-hop politics to have a substantial political impact, the voting bloc should reflect the full range of American youth who identify with this youth culture. The hip-hop voting bloc, then, goes beyond the group of youth described as "the hip-hop generation" to include those individuals, regardless of race, age or sex, who helped make 50 Cent's *Get Rich or Die Tryin'* sell 800,000 copies in its first week or Kanye West's *College Dropout* sell over 400,000 units its first week or Eminem sell 1.7 million copies of the *Marshall Mathers* LP when it debuted. Hip-hop's voting bloc is not limited to a rap music–buying audience but is composed of young people (from 18 to 40-something) whose hip-hop sensibility goes beyond simply being consumers. Understanding the hip-hop voting bloc requires one to consider a world of hip-hop that more often than not goes far beyond the confines of the ways hip-hop is most often publicly discussed— as music or as pop culture alone. To comprehend the hip-hop voting bloc, then, requires one to think of hip-hop as a cultural phenomenon that began as an influential local force in Black communities but now captures the imagination of youth across racial, ethnic and geographic boundaries. As a culture, in the community and beyond, hip-hop has its own value system, along with spiritual, political and economic imperatives that can't be defined by pop music alone.

Consider the statistics. Nineteen million voters out of the 45 million eligible voters aged 18–35 voted in 2000, according to Rock the Vote. The Census Bureau reported that 35 percent of eighteen- to twenty-five-year-old Americans voted in 2000, the lowest percentage ever for this age-group. According to the Joint Center, 13 percent of eighteen- to twenty-five-year-old Black Americans voted in 2000. As these statistics indicate, at least half of those in this age-group, as well as those into their early forties who identify with hip-hop, have stayed away from the polls—until now. Separate surveys conducted before fall 2004 by both the Harvard Institute of Politics and the Pew Research Center concluded that young voters would turn out in record numbers for the 2004 presidential election. More than 20 million eighteen- to twenty-nine-year-olds voted for president in 2004, according to Associated Press exit polls. According to the Center for Information and Research on Civic Engagement at the University of Maryland, voter turnout also increased for other age-groups, leaving young voters with the same percentage of the electorate.

Significant to this hip-hop voting bloc are young white Americans. It can be argued that there will be no substantial hip-hop political movement that doesn't include white hip-hop kids. Why? First, as young Blacks remain a minority in a majority-rule government, coalition politics is essential to moving any "Black" agenda. Second, coalition politics is essential to hip-hop's political possibilities because American racial politics over the past three or four decades has consistently refused to address the crises facing Black youth, including education, poverty, employment, incarceration and health care, to name a few. If these crises aren't connected in a meaningful way to a social agenda beyond Black youth alone, then correcting them will become increasingly difficult. Finally, although young whites may or may not be hip-hop's dominant audience, they do represent a sizable audience. And increasingly this audience, given the shifting economy of the past two decades, finds greater parity with its Black and Latino counterparts than with corporate, elite agendas—whether Democrat or Republican.

White Hip-Hop Activism

The terms "hip-hop activist" and "hip-hop politics" only emerged in the past five to seven years. These expressions were Black activists' way to distinguish our generation's activist work from that of the civil rights/Black power era, a way of indicating to our peers that we were not pursuing what we have collectively concluded are outdated, nonworking models for mobilizing youth and transforming our communities. Instead, we are exploring new methods and strategies informed by the past generation's experiences but closer to the resolve, innovation, sensibility and worldview that youth put into creating our generation's music. Hence the expressions "raptivist" and "rap activism" in the early to mid-1990s and later "hip-hop activism" were born.

To date, much of the commentary on hip-hop activism has focused primarily on Black and Latino youth and to a lesser extent Native Americans and Asian Americans (who are too often lumped in with Blacks and Latinos under a vague "people of color" banner). Entirely missing from the equation is the world of young whites who engage in hip-hop activism. What are the issues that matter to young white hip-hop activists? How does their agenda differ from that of young white conservatives? Do the strategies of young white progressives vastly differ from those of young white liberals who deem themselves hip-hop activists? What about young white liberals and progressives who avoid hip-hop–specific activism altogether? Are young white hip-hop activists even bound by these categories? Do they traverse liberal, progressive, conservative and hip-hop activism? The answers to these questions are crucial to understanding ways that white youth's love for hip-hop, more often than not, extends beyond music and pop culture to the political arena.

Before we can understand the intricacies of white hip-hop activism, one major misconception about hip-hop activism needs to be clarified. There is the tendency in mainstream discourse to define hip-hop and discuss its activism as a youth-only phenomenon. Hip-hop is the youth culture of the generation that came of age in the 1980s and 1990s. Hip-hop generationers at the older end of the age-group are well into their thirties. And those in their early forties, who technically fall into the baby boom generation but identify with hip-hop, should not be overlooked. Many of them helped usher in the hip-hop explosion and turned on many younger hip-hop kids to activism. Lisa Sullivan, founder of LISTEN, Inc., defined those folks as the "bridge generation." (I discuss this bridge generation in *The Hip-Hop Generation*.) Hip-hop pioneers like Afrika Bambaataa and Grandmaster Flash, writers like Nelson George and Greg Tate and activists like Lisa Sullivan and DeLacy Davis (founder of Black Cops Against Police Brutality) all fall into the bridge years, technically in the civil rights generation but functioning between the civil rights generation and the hip-hop generation. They were responsible in many ways for nurturing our generation's political focus.

Relative to the Black community, hip-hop is "youth" culture to the extent that it is juxtaposed to the Black cultural identity ascribed to by older Blacks (baby boomers born between 1945 and 1964, and World War II generationers born between 1925 and 1944). Of course there are Black cultural elements shared by younger and older Blacks. Also there are Black youth–specific variables that unify young people but are not shared by older Blacks. ("Get money," for example, is as central to the hip-hop generation as social uplift is to the civil rights generation.) To escape the idea that hip-hop culture is limited to teenagers, think of "civil rights culture" as the Black youth culture of the 1950s and early 1960s and "Black power culture" as the Black youth culture of the late 1960s and early 1970s. Both were generation-specific cultures that evolved out of the circumstances of their time—not necessarily youth-specific culture. The fact that advocates of civil rights and Black power outgrew their youthful exuberance and inexperience, for example, does not negate their generation-specific cultural worldview.

Likewise, even though hip-hop is the youth culture of young Blacks who came of age in the 1980s and 1990s, it is still relevant to youth now in their twenties, teens and younger because of the tremendous influence of popular culture. For many who fall into what has been described as the millennium generation (those born between 1985 and 2004), especially those at the end and middle of the age-group, hip-hop has defined the circumference of their lives. Hakim of the hip-hop group Channel Live, describing the influence of hip-hop on the hip-hop generation, put it this way: "Rap music is what you hear on the radio and see in music videos. Hip-hop, on the other hand, is how we survived the anti-youth public policy of the '80s and '90s." Hip-hop culture is having a similar effect on the millennium generation, although that generation may yet evolve a youth culture of its own. For now, the post-hip-hop millennium generation more often than not identifies with a hip-hop culture that is a merging of mainstream pop culture with the local manifesta- tions of hip-hop's cultural movement (local mixtape deejays, emcees, spoken work artists, graffiti artists, party promoters etc.) that operate separately from the corporate-controlled hip- hop music industry.

White hip-hop activists fall into two main categories: (1) those who were activists first, or at least were activist minded, and later connected with hip-hop's emerging political movement either through student activism, grassroots activism or elec- toral politics work, and (2) those who moved in the opposite direction; they were involved in the hip-hop arts world and from there made the leap to political activism as the natural progression of their evolving engagement with race—hip-hop being a natural gateway to activism.

"People who may get into the hip-hop underground in- evitably take the next step," says Mattie Weiss, 25, who grew up in an activist family. "Now that you've made a critique of society, what are you going to do about it?" Weiss was a stu- dent activist first and later made the connection to hip-hop. "I love politics and I love understanding the world in a political way. That's why I love hip-hop. Artists are saying in the music what I already believe. For me, the politics were already there. Then I found hip-hop."

When it comes to white hip-hop activists, just as in the Black and Latino hip-hop communities, there are at least two generations of activists within the hip-hop generation age-group. The older activists—those in their mid-thirties to early forties—generally became engaged in activism back in the day before people referred to hip-hop activism as such. These were individuals who were activists and happened to fall into the hip-hop generation age-group. In the early days, their activism was not defined by hip-hop. Hip-hop as a cultural movement was still unfolding, including any hip-hop generation-specific activism. Thus many of these activists, like their hip-hop arts counterparts (politically conscious rappers like Chuck D, KRS-One, Poor Righteous Teachers, X-Clan, Brand Nubian, Queen Latifah and even those who weren't necessarily identified as conscious but leaned that way), identified with 1960s and 1970s activists and causes and their holdovers. Despite helping politicize the hip-hop generation, these artists and activists, Black and white, had yet to define hip-hop generation–specific issues and activism. Gradually they began to hone in on a hip-hop generation-specific activism replete with its own set of issues, including paramilitary policing, education crises, inadequate McJobs, unaffordable housing, nearly nonexistent economic infrastructure in urban and rural communities and so on.

Another important distinction is that most white hip-hop activists see a radical analysis of race at the forefront of their engagement with other social and political issues. Such an analysis is paramount in what distinguishes them as white hip-hop activists, as opposed to liberals, conservatives and to a lesser extent progressives. These activists are also working more closely with their Black counterparts than their parents' generation did. Weiss, whose parents were involved in national and international activism in the 1960s, described it this way: "My dad said to me that the younger generation has a better sense of how to organize with each other around coalition building. 'You all have a multiracial camaraderie that we never had,' he says. 'We made like we were down with the Panthers, but we didn't know anything about them personally.'"

Some are what I call children of the white left. Their parents were activists and their analysis progresses naturally out of how they were reared to engage race, class and gender. Some are working class, some middle class. Most are well educated. Others are privileged white kids who have seen the contradictions of the older generation, its activists included, and the divide between what they practice and what they preach. These contradictions appear most forcefully in their own parents. Indoctrinated as children to believe the dream of universal brotherhood and an "e pluribus unum" America, they see the myth-defying reality and are ashamed of it. Most recognize white privilege as a significant part of the problem and dismantling it as part of the solution. They focus their activism on constructing strategies to fight against it. Some are getting involved at a national level for the first time via organizations like the League of Pissed Off Voters because they see it as the first real vehicle that makes sense to their generation-specific worldview.

The issues that concern white hip-hop activists are mostly the same ones that matter to youth across the board (living wage jobs, military-industrial complex, education, environment and incarceration). So there are plenty of possibilities for an effective cross-racial coalition.

In the early days, white hip-hop activism was limited to the hip-hop industry. Activists attempted to dismantle the music industry's long-standing system of exploitation, as it affected their favorite hip-hop artists. For some white hip-hop activists, it was the lyrics and oppositional politics of hip-hop artists that were directly responsible for waking them up to American democracy's many brutal contradictions. Rather than work directly on grassroots activist issues, they focused on racism, classism and sexism in the hip-hop industry.

Among those pioneers leading the charge was Wendy Day, the Harriet Tubman of hip-hop activism, who has led many Black rap artists to the promised land of financially solvent record deals. Born and raised in a middle-class Philadelphia family (postal worker dad, stay-at-home mom), Day didn't get involved in activism until after graduate school. Her parents weren't activists, but she was always motivated by injustice. She credits Molefi Asante, the father of Afrocentricity (whom she studied under to obtain a master's degree in African American studies in the 1980s), with teaching her to view the world from "an Afrocentric perspective." She formed the Rap Coalition in 1992 after taking an accounting course at New York University. The professor spent several days lecturing about the raw deal too many rap artists were receiving from their corporate record labels. Day was amazed that no one would fight for them.

Day raised the funds to start the Rap Coalition by liquidating all of her assets, including her condominium and BMW. At 42, she's still giving record executives nightmares, in addition to helping artists create structures independent of the mainstream industry.

Billy Wimsatt, who would later help found the influential and visionary League of Pissed Off Voters and played a role in the National Hip-Hop Political Convention, was also on the front lines of white hip-hop activism. Wimsatt came up in hip-hop as graffiti artist Upski in Chicago's underground scene. When breathing paint fumes and bombing trains got old to his teenaged-turned-twenty-something body, Wimsatt started writing about hip-hop, offering some of the first hip-hop commentary that challenged white hip-hop kids to avoid exploiting Black culture. He later turned the essay into a short, sweet and influential book, *Bomb the Suburbs* (1994), in which he insists that white hip-hop kids had more of an obligation than to simply be culture bandits.* Rather, they were called to give back to hip-hop as much or more than they were taking from it. It's a position he

---

*Not unlike the way Day and Wimsatt entered hip-hop activism, Danny Hoch stayed close to hip-hop's cultural roots, advancing a type of art as weapon of resistance approach that has deep roots in international freedom movements. Born in 1970, Hoch grew up in Queens in the 1980s and 1990s under the influence of hip-hop. Dabbling in graffiti art and break dancing, he began to think through the contradictions of race and class in mainstream culture. Hoch took the same perspective as Wimsatt and Day to the performing arts world, as a performer, an activist and a critic. By the early 1990s, when his one-man play *Jail, Hospitals, Hip-hop* began touring the country, he was already a household name among hip-hop heads for his outspoken criticism of America's old racial politics. In his one-man plays *(Pot Melting, Some People)*, on the big screen *(Bamboozled, Black Hawk Down)* and as a writer *(White Boyz)* Hoch has a threefold mission: (1) to get people to see that the art and culture play a role in the political reality, (2) to bring awareness to the fact that Americans across race have more in common than the old racial politics is willing to admit and (3) to challenge both in writing, in his creative art, and in the roles he chooses or refuses to play on film, the contemporary artist's responsibility to intervene to disrupt the old racial politics— whether advanced by corporate structures or everyday people.

feels even stronger about after jumping in the trenches to do his part to bridge the gap between hip-hop and electoral politics.

"I feel like white people are too quick to opt out. They don't put in that much effort to organize across race. They feel like they are putting in a lot, but in the grand scheme of things it's a token amount. It's not putting much on the line in comparison to what others have on the line without a choice. The result is like anything you don't fully commit to—a half-ass relationship."

Wimsatt, like Day, isn't shy about putting his money where his mouth is. When I ask Day if there's a difference in the work of white and Black hip-hop activists, say, Billy Wimsatt and Donna Frisby Greenwood, the former coexecutive director of Rock the Vote, her reflections mirror Billy's thinking about the distance whites must go to make cross-racial coalitions work. "Billy can go home and Donna can't," she says. "Billy grew up in a world where he was taught to be intelligent and to question authority as part of the culture. Donna's lived her life as an African American female. Billy can go home anytime he wants to. He can go work on Wall Street and make $3 million a year. At the end of the day, he can say, 'This isn't my life; I'm just fighting for what I *feel* is right.' Donna is home. As a white hip-hop activist even on a daily basis when I climb into my car and drive home at the end of the day, I'm not stopped by the police. I'm not going to be arrested for drugs. Women don't clutch their purses when they see me. Billy's activism is based on what he *sees* as unjust. Donna's is based on what she's *lived* as unjust."

Although most white hip-hop activism has been local, three prominent exceptions were the cutting-edge college student hip-hop conferences—Words, Beats, Life at the University of Maryland; The Hip-Hop Generation at the University of Wisconsin-Madison and the San Jose State University Hip-Hop Congress. Notably all of these were cross-cultural student activist attempts at organizing the hip-hop generation, a common characteristic of a fair number of hip-hop clubs on college campuses. These efforts are vulnerable to the usual problems facing college activism in general, but they are the only show in town, on or off campus. Outside of the college setting, only recently have there been attempts to take local and regional efforts to a national level.

Organizing the Hip-Hop Voting Bloc Across Race

At the Museum of Science in Industry in Chicago in the fall of 2003, a conference entitled Hip-Hop and Social Change brought together hip-hop activists, practitioners and theorists from around the world. The question posed to one panel on hip-hop activism was, "What are some current examples of coalition building?" No one could answer, but in fact two national efforts were already under way: the first ever National Hip-Hop Political Convention and the League of Pissed Off Voters.

Conceived in March 2003, the National Hip-Hop Political Convention sought to tap into the existing informal infrastructure created by hip-hop's cultural movement. Its organizers aimed to help hip-hop activists begin to network nationally, gain a national voice in the process and ultimately transform our cultural leverage into political power. To do this, informal local networks of party promoters, independent artists, aspiring artists, party goers, street teams, hip-hop activists, spoken word poets, local political operatives, hip-hop journalists, radio personalities and the like, were encouraged to formalize their associations. Out of those more concrete gatherings came local organizing committees that registered voters and sent delegates to represent local interests at the national convention. Once at the convention the delegates voted on and endorsed a national hip-hop political agenda. By the time the convention convened in Newark in June 2004, a more cohesive national network of hip-hop generation individuals and organizations had emerged in local, regional and national settings.* Although the National Hip-Hop Political Convention made an appeal to white hip-hop activists, the leadership was heavily Black, with some Latino, white and Asian involvement. The convention turnout reflected this. There were over 3,000 attendees and approximately 400 delegates, with roughly 10–15 percent white representation. Many of the white participants were members of the League of Pissed Off Voters.

From the start, the League of Pissed Off Voters had a more diverse racial and ethnic composition, not only among the rank and file but also in its leadership, which includes women, Blacks, Latinos and whites. By the time the Chicago Hip-Hop and Social Change conference met in 2003, the League of Pissed

---

*Several local and regional spin-off conventions followed. Ohio NHHPC participants held a statewide debriefing meeting weeks after the national convention. The New York City local organizing committee for the NHHPC called a gathering of area hip-hop activist groups a month after the NHHPC. Similar gatherings took place in Pittsburgh (a statewide event) and Oakland.

Off Voters had already hit the ground running. The League is an umbrella group formed in 2003 to govern the activities of three main organizations: the League of Young Voters, the League of Pissed Off Voters and the League of Independent Voters. The League works with existing local and national organizations to train 18- to 30-year-olds how to get involved in the political process. The organization does this through a variety of training events such as Smackdown 2004, a national political convention that convened in Columbus, Ohio, in July 2004.

The League uses the Internet (Indyvoter.org and Pissed voter.org) in addition to a variety of outreach methods to create local "progressive" voting guides, scorecards and endorsement slates. By the 2004 election, the group had twenty-five chapters around the country. Operatives in each community create scorecards and endorsement slates on local, state and national candidates, posted them on the Internet and canvassed communities seeking commitments from individuals to vote the slate in their local areas. Operating on the principle that all politics is local, the League intends to get youth involved in electoral politics by building local voting blocs that will hold politicians accountable.

The League set a target of 1 million votes for the slate in 2004. In an attempt to solidify the organization's identity, it published a book called *How to Get Stupid White Men Out of Office*, an anthology that documents fifteen elections in which 18- to 30-year-olds were the decisive swing vote. Relative to the presidential election, they capitalized on dissatisfaction with the U.S. war with Iraq alongside President Bush's domestic economic policies to draw young people to the

cause. One of its most innovative projects was a series of emcee battles around the country called SlamBush, where local
rap artists and spoken word poets were invited to spit their
most clever rhyme about the president.* SlamBush culminated with a national competition in Miami, Florida, weeks
before the election.

In the spring of 2004, after the smoke cleared from the Democratic presidential primary and John Kerry was all but for-
mally nominated as the Democratic candidate, the Young Voter
Alliance emerged. The Alliance targeted the hip-hop voting
bloc as a way of bringing enough votes to the Democratic Party
to win the election. "This year, young people will swing the
election for the Democrats through the Young Voter Alliance,"
its Web site proclaimed. "Our mission in 2004 is to make young
voters the swing voters needed to elect progressives up and
down the ticket in our target states." Like other nonprofit
groups known as 527s that emerged at the same time, YVA
sought to take advantage of a loophole in the Bipartisan Campaign Reform Act of 2002. The 527 nonprofits became a haven
for the unlimited soft money that had been outlawed by campaign finance reform. The Young Voter Alliance rode the mo-

---

*SlamBush was the brainchild of Hip-Hop Renaissance man Davey D
Cook. Davey D was one of the contributors to *How to Get Stupid White
Men Out of Office*. Deejay, journalist, hip-hop politics commentator, one
of the organizers of the National Hip-Hop Political Convention and
more, Davey D has served as one of the unsung guardian angels of the
marriage between hip-hop and politics—from maintaining his Web site
to linking folks in both worlds to offering brilliant strategies as well as
implementing them.

mentum of hip-hop and politics that was being generated by
the Hip-Hop Summit Action Network, the upcoming National
Hip-Hop Political Convention, the formation of P. Diddy's Citizen Change and the noise being made by the League of Pissed
Off Voters. The Young Voter Alliance furthered two ideas that
were close to the League's vision: organizing across race and
concentrating on swing voters. Conceptually the Young Voter
Alliance was even more diverse than the League. The Alliance
called on the five existing founding organizations (The League
of Pissed Off Voters, Young Democrats of America, The League
of Hip-Hop Voters, The Stonewall Student Network and U.S.
Student Association) to work collectively to get out the hip-hop
vote (what they defined as 18- to 30-five-year-olds) for Democratic candidates in five swing states—Ohio, Florida, Wis-
consin, New Mexico and Pennsylvania. The group aimed to
increase new voters by 3 percent, a margin it claimed would
have been enough to clinch the 2000 presidential election. With
the inclusion of the Stonewall Student Network—the youth di-
vision of the gay, lesbian, bisexual and transgender Stonewall
Democrats—as a founding member, the Young Voter Alliance's
vision for a coalition went beyond race.

But perhaps more central to the group's calling was its attempt to reach the hard-core hip-hop vote, particularly young
Black and Latino voters, known to be less likely than their
parents to vote for Democratic candidates as a matter of principle. The Alliance deployed tactics traditionally used by mar-
keters and hip-hop promoters to reach hip-hop voters and
claimed to be creating a "new voter model" to reach young
first-time voters.

Rather than create a model for hip-hop activists who would delve into electoral politics, however, the group seemingly tried to patent already existing links between hip-hop activism, hip-hop arts and an emerging hip-hop politics. Such a patent would give electoral politics insiders a blueprint for reaching the hip-hop voting bloc. To quote again from its Web site: "The New Voter Model will incorporate multiple peer-to-peer contacts (local face, local message), a sense of national momentum, and connect voting to the issues that young people care about." What this approach overlooked was that similar models had already been implemented around the country by numerous informal collectives of hip-hop activists, artists and political operatives—even if it lacked an official seal. Examples abound from the Hip-Hop Political Action Committee in Chicago to BUILD (Blacks United in Search of Local Democracy) in Cleveland to the Get on the Bus Project in Portland. Much of this is sporadic and differs slightly depending on regional needs.

In this regard, YVA put the cart before the horse, responding to the needs of the Democratic Party for a hip-hop vote initiative, instead of striking a balance between local needs and mainstream political aims. YVA and similar get-out-the-hip-hop-vote efforts, intentionally or not, helped set the wheels in motion for the emerging hip-hop political movement to be pimped by the Democrats. "They are using the hip-hop network—which is basically a group of independents—to gain access to eighteen- to thirty-five-year-olds," said one Ohio hip-hop organizer who worked directly with such organizers in that battleground state. "I'm from the streets. Game recognize game. This is just another hustle."

The League doesn't quite view it that way. From where it sits, it's the Democratic Party that's subject to being took. "This is a tactical alliance with the Democrats to beat Bush," Billy Wimsatt said. "What people aren't getting is that things could be worse." For now, the League is building voter blocs and hoping to swing future elections. Long term, the group believes it can move into the Democratic Party ranks and become a strong enough force to bring about change in the years ahead, as America's minority becomes the majority. "If we can stop the Republicans now," Wimsatt said before the election, "every two years things get better for building a progressive majority. The Democratic Party is not a giant in the hillside. It can be taken over by any strong group of people. The left has to do a lot of the things that the right has done, which is to build a left wing of the Democratic Party. That's our best shot right now: take over the Democratic Party and steer it left in a way that won't alienate people and in a way that is bold and visionary."

The Young Voter Alliance, the League of Young Voters, and the National Hip-Hop Political Convention are off to a great start. They go the distance in creating a necessary local and regional counterbalance to hip-hop's foray into electoral politics by prominent, celebrity-driven groups like the Hip-Hop Summit Action Network and Citizen Change. Their flaws were magnified in part because these were all youth-oriented organizations that dared emerge in an election year. The National Hip-Hop Political Convention, for example, was criticized for creating excitement but lacking an organizational structure for follow-through. The NHHPC was a loose coalition of organizations and individuals with an army of ideologies and sometimes subtle differences about the best strategy for achieving hip-hop voting bloc influence. Although the collective was committed to future conventions, it lacked coordinated movement around an election strategy, leaving many involved to fall into other efforts: the Kerry or Bush campaigns or get out the vote initiatives of the YVA, the League, the Hip-Hop Civic Engagement Project or their own local efforts.* For success in the long run, they must build on the best of past efforts. Attempts at organizing across race aren't new and hip-hop's emerging political movement needn't reinvent the wheel.

From Harold Washington to Hip-Hop

In 1984 Jesse Jackson's Rainbow Coalition strategy—the only national effort to date with any degree of success—emerged as the backbone of Jackson's presidential campaign. The Rainbow Coalition was improved four years later when Jackson again entered the Democratic primaries. In 1983, a year before Jackson popularized the idea of a rainbow coalition, Harold Washington's campaign for mayor of Chicago made a stunning display of coalition politics.** Washington was easily reelected in 1987, after using a similar approach and having delivered on

---

*The second National Hip-Hop Political Convention is slated for Chicago in June 2006.

**The term "rainbow coalition" had its roots with famed Chicago Black Panther Fred Hampton, who worked to build coalitions across race in the late 1960s.

the promise of a coalition government during his first adminis-tration. In some ways, Harold Washington's mayoral campaign, as well as Jackson's 1984 presidential campaign, grew out of the Gary, Indiana, National Black Political Convention of 1972.* Two variables worked for both the Washington coalition and Jackson's Rainbow Coalition: a large bloc of disaffected voters, many of whom were first-time voters, and multiethnic and multiracial coalitions that came together around common in-terests. Both variables are strongly present in the emerging hip-hop political movement.

Many of Washington's core Black supporters hadn't voted before because they felt the process was bankrupt and they

---

*After Fred Hampton and Mark Clark were assassinated by Chicago po-lice in a raid planned by Cook County state's attorney Edward Hanrahan, Blacks voted Hanrahan out of office in 1972—the same year as the Gary, Indiana, National Black Political Convention. Gary Rivlin refers to Han-rahan's involvement in planning the raid on Fred Hampton and Mark Clark and the community mobilization to remove him from office in the aftermath in his *Fire on the Prairie* as one of the early organizing efforts in the Black community that would later assist the Harold Washington election effort. Some of this energy coming out of Chicago went to the Gary convention. Gary is a stone's throw away from Chicago's south and west sides, which have the highest concentration of Blacks in the city. In 1967 Gary elected its own Black mayor, Richard Hatcher, who hosted the convention, spearheaded in some respects by Amiri Baraka—coming on the heels of the election of Ken Gibson in Newark in 1970, in which Baraka played a crucial role. Komozi Woodard, professor of American history at Sarah Lawrence College, documents Baraka's role in both and gives one of the most detailed analyses to date of the Gary, Indiana, Black Political Convention in his *A Nation Within a Nation: Amiri Baraka and Black Power Politics* (1999).

could have a more meaningful impact working at a grassroots community level. At the same time those working within the system (Blacks, whites and others) were crucial to Washington's success, as the million-strong Chicago Black community represented a sizable base but only about 35 percent of the total population. Another important part of Washington's focus was an appeal to break the stranglehold of the Chicago Democratic Party machine. In the early 1980s Chicago was the only major city that still had a nineteenth-century-style political machine. "The Cook County Democratic machine thrived long after machines were no longer supposed to function," writes Gary Rivlin in *Fire on the Prairie: Chicago's Harold Washington and the Politics of Race* (1992, p. 4). "When famous urban cousins like New York's Tammany Hall had gone the way of the icebox, the Chicago organization hadn't even reached its peak."

Many of Washington's coalition constituents were those locked out of the Democratic machine's good ol' boy network: the young, the poor, the disenfranchised, whites, Blacks, Latinos and women. Rivlin described Washington's coalition this way: "There were those who saw themselves as part of a Black liberation movement and others as part of an antimachine crusade. Still others were drawn to the campaign of a candidate to the left of liberal. Yet they all saw enough of themselves in Washington to ensure they all shared a stake in his election" (p. 138).

When Jesse Jackson sought the Democratic nomination for president in 1984, he took Washington's coalition strategy to a national level. Although the Rainbow Coalition merged with Jackson's Operation PUSH to form Rainbow/PUSH in 1996, the Rainbow Coalition between the 1984 and 1988 campaigns was a vastly different animal. Jackson's 1984 campaign registered over a million voters, and the 1988 campaign registered over 2 million. Part of what made Jackson so successful was his appeal to a multiethnic and multiracial coalition across race, class and gender that, just like Washington's coalition, was all inclusive—Black Americans, Latinos, Asian Americans, Arab Americans, Native Americans, new young voters, labor, working poor, struggling middle class, women, gays and lesbians and disabled veterans.

In his address at the 1984 Democratic National Convention, Jesse Jackson described the Rainbow Coalition as a quilt.

America is not like a blanket—one piece of unbroken cloth, the same color, the same texture, the same size. America is more like a quilt: many patches, many pieces, many colors, many sizes, all woven and held together by a common thread. The white, the Hispanic, the black, the Arab, the Jew, the woman, the Native American, the small farmer, the businessperson, the environmentalist, the peace activist, the young, the old, the lesbian, the gay and the disabled make up the American quilt.

Even in our fractured state, all of us count and fit somewhere. We have proven that we can survive without each other. But we have not proven that we can win and make progress without each other. We must come together.

In a recent editorial looking back on the impact of the Rainbow Coalition, Ron Daniels, former executive director of the National Rainbow Coalition and deputy campaign manager of the 1988 Jackson for President campaign, described Jackson's coalition this way:

> Rev. Jesse Jackson articulated a program of social and economic justice that was calculated to neutralize and nullify the "divide and exploit" strategy that various elements of the power elite have used historically to drive a wedge between the races. His message of "economic common ground" was the foundation for the Rainbow Coalition as a vehicle that could bring together diverse racial groups and issue constituencies under one umbrella. The Rainbow Coalition created a space where Red, Yellow, Brown, Black and White, labor, environmentalist and peace activists, women, youth, lesbian and gay. . . could all come together to forge a united front to pursue their interest and the quest for transforming America. (August 22, 2004, The Black World Today Web site, www.tbwt.com)

Jackson's coalition, to a greater extent than Washington's, relied on a white majority, as over 75 percent of Americans in 1984, according to the U.S. Census Bureau, were white. In addition, it had a national scope as opposed to a city landscape, which forced a radically different dynamic than the one Washington was facing. What should not be forgotten in assessing the Rainbow Coalition's impact is that Jackson never held political office at any level. This was the blind faith that voters across race, class and gender bought into. These variables alone made Jackson's coalition a much harder sell. To the extent that it was successful against these odds, including voters' willingness to raise the old racial politics and embrace a Black candidate, suggests the possibilities for a rainbow coalition in a hip-hop era.

In the end, the old racial politics prevailed. Part of the Rainbow Coalition's success lay in the belief that if the Democratic Party wouldn't deliver on issues that mattered to various constituencies, then Jackson was prepared to go a third way, either in forming another political party or at least a third major force having a voice and exerting influence. Jackson's decision to cast his lot with the Democratic Party ultimately sealed the fate of the coalition. By 1996, when PUSH and the Rainbow Coalition merged, the coalition constructed in the 1980s had come and gone.

Although Harold Washington successfully practiced coalition politics in governing Chicago for one term, his political movement unfortunately ended with his death a few months into his second term. But his campaign, as well as Jackson's, underscores the strengths and shortcomings of coalition politics. This is where a hip-hop political movement really begins—where Harold Washington's and Jesse Jackson's coalition movements end.

Some Black political theorists, such as Ron Walters of the University of Maryland, have argued that to some extent, the election of Jimmy Carter in 1976, Bill Clinton in 1992 and 1996 and even Al Gore's winning the popular vote in 2000, all relied

on swing votes of Black Americans.* Yet Blacks had little influence, even during the Clinton administrations. Actually, Blacks
suffered setbacks (rising incarceration rates, new mandatory
minimums and welfare reform were the big ones) on the
watch of the so-called first Black president. The New Democrat Clinton, for sure, gave us Black faces in high places—Ron
Brown, Alexis Herman, Vernon Jordan, to name a few—but
this Black cabinet didn't provide far-reaching access in terms
of influencing a Black political agenda. Worse still, the Clinton
approach set the stage for President George W. Bush and his
neoconservative associates to perfect the formula in constructing a Black cabinet of their own with Secretary of State Colin
Powell, national security adviser Condoleezza Rice, and education secretary Rod Paige, individuals with more allegiance to
President Bush than to a Black voting bloc's political agenda.
As the clock turned back on civil rights, racial politics and all
aspects of a progressive agenda between 1984 and 2004, it became clear that any coalition politics of substance ended with
the Rainbow Coalition 1988 effort. The political activity (or
inactivity) of these two decades also raises questions about the
current emerging hip-hop voting bloc leadership, which seems
to be on a path to repeat this history, especially since the get-
out-the-hip-hop-vote efforts overwhelmingly support the
Democratic Party. With these concerns in mind, how do we in
hip-hop's emerging political movement take these promising
coalition efforts to the next level?

---

*In a presentation at the 2004 Black Political Agenda Coordinating Com-
mittee meeting in Chicago at Chicago State University, July 19, 2004.

Six Obstacles to Organizing Across Race

As a country we haven't taken the next step. The emerging hip-hop political movement is in a unique position to serve as a catalyst for doing so, especially given (1) the institutionalization of civil rights rhetoric in America's mainstream, from high school textbooks to congressional rhetoric; (2) the impact of an ever-shifting economy that is increasingly bringing young whites face-to-face with realities facing people of color, regardless of class—with American poverty growing across race into the twenty-first century and the outsourcing of white- and blue-collar jobs; and (3) the impact of hip-hop culture and Black popular culture in general, from music and film, comedy to sports, on the younger generation. Yet obstacles to organizing across race persist, more often than not steeped in the old racial politics. A brief overview of hip-hop activism as it intersected with get-out-the-vote efforts of 2004 suggest some of the obstacles that may lie ahead. Here are six to consider.

1. A Blacks-only-identified hip-hop political movement. We need to construct a new language for discussing and framing unresolved social issues. The National Hip-Hop Summit Action Network convened twenty-six summits in the 18 months leading up to the election. All were attended mostly by Blacks. The National Hip-Hop Political Convention, despite its appeal to hip-hop voters across race, was heavily "Black" in regard to turnout and issues. For hip-hop's emerging political movement to be effective, a hip-hop voting bloc must frame issues in a way that simultaneously advances the hip-hop agenda and promotes inclusivity. Often this is just semantics. Young whites are becoming as alienated as Blacks from the mainstream. We need to construct a language that speaks to that common ground rather than using the divisive language of the old racial politics. The debate around prisons, for example, is about societal inequity that disproportionately affects Black Americans in terms of actual incarcerations. However, its implications negatively affect all Americans. Political science professor Mark Cassell spearheaded a symposium on prisons at Kent State University in April 2003 entitled Dollars and Sense: The Economics of Criminal Justice Policies. Cassell believes that the mandatory minimum sentencing issue should be reframed as an economics issue. This, he says, would highlight the wide-reaching impact of prisons on both local and national economies. Our unity around the issues may be even more striking when it comes to living-wage jobs, education reform and affordable college tuition.

Hip-hop politics, just like hip-hop music and culture, has an intrinsic appeal to all Americans. If we fail to create a new language for discussing issues once deemed "Black," we will remain prisoners of the old racial politics. Properly reframing the issues can assist the crucial need to build a political movement. This movement must have the potential to morph into a political party that can appeal to Americans regardless of race, class, gender, age or sexual orientation. This cannot be done if hip-hop politics is deemed solely a Black thing.

The National Hip-Hop Political Convention created a five-point national hip-hop agenda that speaks to the issues currently devastating America's young people across the board: education (equal spending in all public schools), human rights (an end to recruitment of our youth into armed forces in public schools and other public institutions), economic justice (investment in underdeveloped neighborhoods and full employment with living-wage jobs), health (free universal health care) and criminal justice (an end to mandatory minimum sentencing). The agenda, which was drafted mostly by Black Americans from twelve states, also speaks to "Black" issues such as reparations. This was more a function of the hip-hop voting bloc's commitment to ending the old racial politics rather than an attempt to be a Black thing.

For the past thirty years, U.S. racial politics, along with globalization, has followed a pattern of "what happens to Blacks today will happen to white youth tomorrow," or next week, or some years down the line. Such was the case of school shootings, failing public education and declining middle-class and working-class employment. So it is not a question of Black Americans compromising their politics to bring whites into the hip-hop politics movement. Rather, those at the forefront of the hip-hop political movement must organize a hip-hop politics around issues affecting *all* American youth—whites, Blacks, Latinos, Asians and Native Americans. The core of the hip-hop bloc's political concern should speak to our common sense of humanity, which hasn't been adequately addressed by our democratic government. Thus a hip-hop politics that makes room for young whites at the table is not about whites adopting a Black-exclusive agenda. Neither is it about whites taking over the movement and Black issues taking a backseat to generic "youth" concerns. Rather, the goal is to correct social ills that are negatively affecting all Americans, including young whites.

Neither Jesse Jackson nor Harold Washington allowed himself to be pigeonholed as a "Black candidate," a euphemism for a candidate who is only concerned with issues that matter to a Black constituency. Jesse Jackson put it this way: "I'm a minority with a majority vision." At the same time neither Jackson nor Washington attempted to "transcend Blackness."

2. The campaign finance reform factor.   During the 2004 campaign, too many hip-hop political organizers got caught up in the money being thrown around by liberal- or progressive-leaning 527 committees. These committees may have hurt hip-hop activist and political efforts as much as they helped. The disruption came in three main forms. First, when the 527 committees jumped into the organizing in swing states, more often than not, the organizing already going on was disrupted. Usually this meant changing the equation by shifting the focus from a hip-hop political agenda to a Democratic Party agenda. Whereas the hip-hop voting bloc should have been concentrating on what it could get out of the election locally and how local organizers wanted to interface with the Democratic Party, now they were following the dictates of the Democratic Party in its quest to win the election. Patronage jobs for hip-hop organizers after the election were rarely considered. Second, the groups often sought to impose an external leadership imported from outside the state rather than work with the local leaders. This didn't mean that local activist leaders weren't called on to be foot-soldiers for the handpicked outsider leadership, just that the local leadership wouldn't be calling the shots. Finally, the 527 equation almost always created a situation where local activists who had been working together for years now found themselves competing for jobs to do the type of work they had already been doing collectively for free. All three forms of disruption are especially problematic for organizers already organized and even more so in the case where local hip-hop activists were still in the early stages of organizing themselves into a cohesive unit with clear goals. This distraction may affect the potential for these groups to organize in the future. When they take money up front in exchange for working on campaigns and get-out-the-vote efforts for the Democratic Party or Democratic-leaning groups, hip-hop political organizers are compromising the hip-hop voting bloc's leverage. Once the campaigning is over and the victory is won, even if the hip-hop vote is a decisive factor in a close margin of victory, where is the commitment by the Democratic Party to a hip-hop voting bloc's political agenda? Because many of these hip-hop activists are being paid for organizing young people who are at least informally organized already, getting on the payroll during an election season seems innocent enough. Indeed it is especially enticing for young people doing political work who need the resources at the personal and organizational levels. However, this type of deal cutting is a trade-off. In most cases, Democratic Party insiders don't feel they owe the hip-hop voting bloc anything. Whatever return we expect has already been spent. This is one of the hard political lessons of 2004 that many, too quick to lead a hip-hop political movement, still haven't come to grips with.

3. In-fighting. A desire to be *the* Black leader persists among some Black Americans. This in turn leads to the "crabs in the bucket" syndrome—a willingness to distrust each other, throw in the towel at the first hint of trouble and vehemently fight it out among ourselves rather than confront a common enemy. Despite hip-hop's success in creating a unified national youth culture, young Black America is not a monolith. A wide variety of political pespectives abound, some inherited from previous movements, some hybrids of past and present. With such a broad spectrum of ideas, there are bound to be clashes, but too many hip-hop activists fail to keep the clashes in check.

Take the first ever National Hip-Hop Political Convention as an example. It was an opportunity to use hip-hop as a tool for political change that attempted to work across race. The group organized around a "leaderless leadership" model that sought collective decisionmaking around key issues, especially ideological ones. Consequently leaders emerged who were excited by the prospects and refused to be accountable to the group. When they forged ahead creating alliances without everyone on board, they ultimately undermined the possibilities. In the heat of battle, one of the organizers said, "As far as I'm concerned, the white man has won," employing a term that activists long have used as a catchall phrase for America's shortcomings. Others, like Ras Baraka, chair of the Newark Convention, repeatedly tried to keep the peace. He reiterated his concern at a press conference in Washington, D.C., where the agenda of the National Hip-Hop Political Convention was officially announced. "As a community, we still don't have the sophistication to say we are going to work together for common good—whether we agree or not." Too many Black hip-hop political organizers don't have it together enough even within our own organizaations to begin to think about ways of creating effective coalitions. Some of our organizations are so young that they are still going through growing pains. Others are simply dysfunctional. Even when we do have it together, we allow our egos to get the best of us as fighting each other consumes the passion, dedication and focus that is needed to build a concrete hip-hop voting bloc. Many of us had hoped that this was a tendency of our parents' generation that we had learned from and left behind. Whites seeking to build coalitions with Black groups need to be aware of this universal human tendency and not allow it to become an excuse for bringing historic paternalistic attitudes into play.

4. Paternalistic attitudes and mainstream attempts to patronize, ghettoize and marginalize the hip-hop vote.   Within the emerging hip-hop political movement some white hip-hop activists, as well as their Black counterparts (who are well-educated about Ivy League power centers but light-years away from a working knowledge of Black communities), descend on the ghetto to save the Blacks. Many of these leading the charge may ape political establishment insiders, often looking to them for clues as to how hip-hop's emerging voting bloc should engage with existing electoral politics (rather than seeking ways to build on that knowledge, adapt it to our needs and rewrite the game). The prevailing wisdom within mainstream political circles is that a political operative or rising star must earn his or her stripes before being entrusted with a leadership post such as heading a get-out-the-vote effort in a swing state. This approach is something that will not fly in the hip-hop activist community. Insiders who would like to help organize a hip-hop voting bloc should be aware of this. To many Black, Latino, Asian and Native American hip-hop voters, this reeks of paternalism rooted in colonialism and perfected in New World slavery—the idea that outsiders know what's better for the natives than the natives themselves. Such paternalism goes beyond race and extends into the idea that big-city dwellers are by nature more savvy and sophisticated at organizing than "the locals." To be effective, any hip-hop activism model must avoid this.

Likewise insulting are attempts by outsiders to "shadow" grassroots activists who are experts in the local terrain, only to subsequently replace the local expert with the outsider who has paid his establishment dues. An imported activist trying to organize the hip-hop voting bloc at the local level is doomed to fail.

The flip side is also true. If hip-hop political activists are to access electoral politics as a tool to ameliorate our communities, hip-hop activists need to gain experience in actual campaigns—no matter how thorough their local knowledge or how tight their local network. It's a classic catch-22. Without experience in actual campaigns, establishment political operatives are reluctant to give local hip-hop activists leadership roles. At the same time, hip-hop activists are reluctant to give away their know-how in exchange for gaining experience on campaigns. Some feel compelled to do so in order to position themselves for the future—next time insiders won't be able to use a lack of experience as an excuse for not empowering local leadership. It's a fine line that many hip-hop activists are forced to walk in 2004.

While white hip-hop activists clamor over organizing the swing state hip-hop vote in the hood in cities like Cleveland, Cincinnati and Columbus, young whites in the Appalachian hills of southern Ohio and rural towns like Elyria and Lorain, Ohio, were left unregistered and unorganized. The question "How is the potential hip-hop voting bloc being nurtured in these areas?" is reportedly asked by Hip-hop political activists like Angela Woodson, cochair of the first National Hip-Hop Political Convention and one of the founders of the Cleveland-based political action committee BUILD. White hip-hop activists like everyone else need to spend quality time swinging votes in their own communities, rather than paternalistically attempting to organize people in urban areas, especially in communities where local hip-hop activists have already organized. In swing states like Ohio, hip-hop activists and many others were literally falling over one another in voter registration and canvassing efforts, with at least twenty-six organizations putting people on the ground to organize the hip-hop voting bloc in Cleveland, Cincinnati and Columbus.* Meanwhile the parents, brothers, sisters, cousins, friends and associates of white hip-hop activists who sit on the fence between liberal and conservative—the true swing voters—were ignored. Who's swinging them?

The call for white hip-hop activists, as well as white liberals and progressives, to focus on their own communities isn't new.

---

*Most of these were flash-in-the-pan efforts out of mainstream existing organizations to have a hip-hop component. Attempts like these to reach the hip-hop voting bloc follow a pattern of tokenization already deployed to win the Black vote, the Latino vote, the veteran vote and so on.

In the 1960s and 1970s activists felt that Black, Latino and Native American activists needed to get "our thing" together before engaging in coalition building. The climate has shifted since that time. As part of an emerging hip-hop voting bloc, Black and Latino hip-hop activists are more organized and are not as needy as some may think. For starters, hip-hop's cultural movement has afforded us a ready infrastructure. Consequently the potential for whites to take over a hip-hop political movement is vastly diminished relative to earlier generations, especially given the skills that many hip-hop activists bring to the table. As the examples cited above indicate, some of us have begun the process of building national organizations and networks. Because these existing organizations and networks are nontraditional, however, the paternalists don't recognize these existing forms as legitimate. Further, they don't acknowledge that local activists have thought through the issues. Theirs is an intellectual arrogance, a ghost of thwarted coalition building in political movements of times past. This call for white hip-hop activists to organize whites is not rooted in fear but in the concern that these communities must be educated on the issues and brought to the table in order to be part of the solution.

5. Democratic and Republican unwillingness to place issues that matter to the hip-hop voting bloc on the national agenda. Where is the national debate on issues that matter to the hip-hop voting bloc? The need to create full employment with living-wage jobs and repeal mandatory minimum sentencing (which criminalizes hundreds of thousands of young people)

is never debated on Capitol Hill on a par with issues like affordable prescription drugs for seniors or same-sex marriage,
which are at the top of the agenda of other voting blocs. Both
major parties pay lip service to hip-hop voting bloc issues, especially during election time, but they are only committed to
baby steps at best—not the giant steps needed to bring about
substantial change in the lives of young people. Considering
the Jackson and Washington campaigns, this argument is at
least twenty years old. Gary Rivlin paraphrases the former
Chicago Tribune columnist Lu Palmer, remarking on why he
stayed out of electoral politics and "stopped voting altogether"
before jumping knee deep into the Harold Washington campaign (and playing a crucial role in building a grassroots base
in the Black community): "Political participation meant the
dumping of one white in favor of another whose political
views were barely distinguishable from his predecessor's."*

The same dilemma persists today. Invigorated by the old
racial politics, Democrats and Republicans have no incentive
to place these issues on the national agenda. In the current climate, they may even find themselves ostracized for attempting to do so. In recent history, especially post–Slick Willie,
Democrats (more so than their Republican counterparts) are
willing at least to *talk* about the issues. We hear all the right
surface commentary on living wage, enough to pull the right
emotional strings to secure votes. But concrete answers get

---

*Lu Palmer's life as a political organizer should be studied by those serious
about building a hip-hop voting bloc. He created and often articulated as
early as 1981 the Washington campaign slogan, "we shall see in 83."

lost in the old unworkable solutions steeped in loose, non-committal jargon like "raising minimum wage" and "creating jobs" rather than a serious discussion of full employment with a living wage. Neither Democrats nor Republicans allowed the 2004 National Hip-Hop Political Agenda to be presented at their convention. Ironically, Republicans at least feigned a willingness to do so.

The inability of these issues to gain a national hearing highlights the compromised condition of American electoral politics. Young voters, especially those between eighteen and twenty-four, have not accumulated enough wealth and political capital to exert influence in today's political landscape. Clearly young people must build an alternate electoral politics infrastructure that goes beyond the existing infrastructure created by hip-hop's cultural movement. We need our own lobby groups, representation in the Senate and the House and a variable in our arsenal to offset the experience of, say, a senator or congressman in office for over twenty years who has all kinds of favors to call in.

As the hip-hop voting bloc ages, a similar vacuum will exist for the next wave of young voters. Part of what makes young people withdraw from the process is not, as the party line of Democrats and Republicans suggests, the fickleness of youth. Rather, youth know coming out the gate that they are at a disadvantage in the process relative to older people. When the older generation does engage young voters, it's mostly in hopes of enlisting youth as foot soldiers in advancing their own special interest agenda. What is needed to make democracy work for young people in America, then, is a process that empowers youth in all of these areas. Perhaps setting aside tax dollars to this end could be a good start. Failing that, how can youth secure resources that will allow them to compete with, say, senior citizens or other special interests groups? Answers may also lie in alternative approaches like proportional representation. In the meantime, as we build a hip-hop voting bloc, we must prioritize nurturing the next generation of young activists, those in the mid to late teens and early twenties.

6. Opportunism.   Hip-hop's emerging political movement must be wary of opportunists who come to the hip-hop political battlefield only to earn the stripes they need to move up the ranks of establishment parties. These opportunists shouldn't be confused with those sincerely committed to building a hip-hop political movement, one that could yield significant results. The establishment field of electoral politics in general is rife with young people trying to make their name. Dues have to be paid. It's far easier to cut one's teeth on the periphery in unexplored terrain, doing hard but useful political work organizing an emerging voting bloc and gaining invaluable political insight and experience, as well as winning new votes useful to the party. The flash-in-the-pan white hip-hop activists who take this approach are assuming a strategy similar to the one advanced by some skilled Black intellectuals who try to separate themselves from the pack of other aspiring intellectuals: write a book about Black people that is full of tough love and parrots all the right conservative talk and concludes that Blacks—not white supremacy, social inequity and poverty are their own worst enemies, need to stop complaining so much about government shortcomings, and pull themselves up by their own bootstraps.*

Not far removed from the stereotypical overnight white hip-hop activists of privileged background are their Black counterparts. Recognizing the untapped monetary value of the work, they are quick to latch onto the hard work of grassroots hip-hop activists who have been laboring on the ground for years. These opportunists take it to the next level and make a hustle of it. Their focus on "getting paid" supersedes the reasons that hip-hop generationers got involved in electoral politics in the first place. Both of these Johnny-come-latelys may have good intentions but need to be checked by grassroots efforts. If hip-hop's political movement is to succeed, bottom-up leadership can't be dismantled when national organizers arrive at local borders. National organizational efforts that espouse bottom-up leadership in theory but come into local communities doing the opposite ultimately do more harm than good. The very presence of opportunists confuse some sincere white hip-hop activists into assuming that all Black hip-hop activists place "getting paid" ahead of the end goals; opportunists also distract sincere young hip-hop activists from exploring new methods of organizing as they adopt mainstream beaten-path approaches. Finally, opportunists threaten to put grassroots hip-hop activists on a mainstream agenda instead of advancing a hip-hop voting bloc political agenda.

---

*John McWhorter (*Losing the Race: Self-Sabatoge in Black America*), Shelby Steele (*The Content of Our Character*), Lawrence Otis Graham (*Our Kind of People*), Keith Richburg (*Out of America: A Black Man Confronts Africa*) and others.

Beware these opportunists, no matter what form they assume. They use efforts to get out the hip-hop vote to tell young people who to vote for, usually Democratic candidates. They have their work cut out for them. Most hip-hop generationers may not be well versed in the language and forms of electoral politics, but they are politically savvy, having been politicized by two decades of public policy that has victimized youth. Those who compose the emerging hip-hop voting bloc are so skeptical about electoral politics to begin with, the last thing most of them want is someone (young or old, insider or outsider) telling them who to vote for. Neither does this approach empower young voters. This voting bloc, like any other, needs leverage. The hip-hop generation's agenda is currently left of both Democrats and Republicans. Until alternative parties and political forces develop clout, it's up to us to motivate existing parties to advance our issues. To get either party to do so, the bloc needs to be able to leverage one against the other. Committing ourselves to the Democratic Party exclusively, as many of these opportunists-activists suggest, squanders that leverage. At the same time, it works against the possibility of a third party or third political force coming into existence in our lifetime.

Again, what the hip-hop voting bloc requires is bottom-up leadership. A hip-hop political movement won't work without clearly formed units (local formal organizations and networks) that understand and have thought through their issues together, who then lobby collectively for their best interests. In 2004 opportunists—with their here-today, gone-tomorrow approach—functioned in a get-Kerry-elected vacuum that ultimately didn't see local organized and informed units as a priority.

The opportunists were quick to sell Democrats (via 527s) the illusion of access to the hip-hop voting bloc, knowing the infrastructure had yet to make the leap from informal to formal. This formal structure cannot be willed into existence. It has to be built. Neither the National Hip-Hop Political Convention nor the League, nor the Young Voter Alliance, nor anyone else to date has done the work in countless communities across the country that needs to be done to transform the informal networks into formal ones. This is a prerequisite to building the type of hip-hop political movement that is needed, especially in a predatory culture where wolves are daily looking for the next hustle. "How can *we* capitalize on this?" is a question folks outside of the hip-hop community have asked about hip-hop even before Sugarhill Gang's "Rapper's Delight" went gold. As we enter the electoral politics game, the stakes become even higher. Add that to the racial politics factor and the odds for another failed political movement—possibly even before it gets off the ground—are vastly multiplied.

Today's political machine is corporate elite free market democracy for the few. And the hip-hop voting bloc—those of us who came of age in America as the global economy went full speed ahead into the new millennium, redefining the American Dream—have a stake in ousting what has become politics as usual. The question is: Is it possible to engage America's so-called minorities in a politics that matters to them, one that offers measurable change, and not create a white backlash in the process, especially as the old racial politics continues to dominate the nation's public political conversation? Can whites believe in Black, Latino, Asian or Native American candidates who are committed to the majority but won't compromise their own cultural integrity as a prerequisite? This means facing the fact that whites—a majority in a majority rules government, alongside a historical racial caste system—had an unfair advantage in the first place. What a working democracy really means in the context of the new racial politics is that whites must "give up" race privilege.

This working democracy includes abandoning the old racial politics, which dismisses any attempt to level the playing field as discrimination against whites. Which brings us back to the Barack Obama phenomenon. Obama's success in the primary and beyond was in many ways dictated by the old racial politics. According to the Joint Center for Political and Economic Studies, for every Black vote he received during the primary, Obama received two from whites. Those white voters, according to pundits, didn't buy into Barack as a "Black" American. As a *New York Times* writer put it ("An Appeal Beyond Race," August 1, 2004), he is Black American by a different set of circumstances, which allow him to—you guessed it—transcend race. "While he is black," writes Scott Malcomson, "he is not the direct product of generations of black life in America: he is not black in the usual way." Or as the *New Republic* ("Race Against History," May 2004) called it, Obama is "an African-American candidate who was not stereotypically African-American," a slick way of calling him the n-word, just not a typical one.

If this is true, whites voting for Obama aren't necessarily moving away from the old racial politics but in fact reinforcing it. These voters are accepting Obama in part because he's

African American only by default. Black in color only not under the influence of African American and world political history. Such rationalization doesn't require white Americans to rethink and abandon the old racial politics—or to part company with white privilege. In the process, it allows them to sidestep the emerging new racial politics. Obama's white supporters in this regard are an aberration. And Obama's success doesn't exactly represent the type of coalition building across race that is needed. This isn't to say that advocates of the new racial politics won't support Obama. But as advocates of the old racial politics back him, the argument will abound that Obama is one of a kind. Without the mixed heritage and immigration ancestry, will other African Americans get similar support? At forty-two Obama is young enough to benefit from a hip-hop voting bloc willing to work across race. At the same time, his mixed-race heritage and immigrant status will certainly appeal to a range of nontraditional voting blocs. However, the terms under which he is "accepted" push back the date for America's arrival in an era when Blacks and other so-called minorities will be electable based on their qualifications and will not have to bury or deny their Blackness to do it. Barack Obama's mainstream reception, as it's being played out, is just more of the same.

Commentators have attempted to distance him from African Americans culturally and politically by honing in on those things he doesn't have in common with African Americans. Such disassociation, they infer, make him more appealing to white voters. This is the same type of distancing that Jesse Jackson was asked to do twenty years earlier, not to be a "Black candidate" but a candidate who happens to be Black. "He did not grow up in a black world and his family had no particular connection to the black experience in America. Yet Obama has black skin and that made him, like it or not, a black man with a place in the centuries-long story of race in America." Malcomson goes on, attempting to distance Obama from his ghetto cousins while ignoring several crucial historical and biographical facts. First, American racism doesn't give Africans or mixed-raced Americans the right to choose whether they will suffer slights because of their Blackness; hence his connection to African Americans "like it or not." Second, Obama's wife is African American. And third, Obama's political mentor is Emil Jones, an Illinois state senator who is Black. Obama's point that he didn't talk about his mother's whiteness in his memoir, *Dreams of My Father*, because he feared "ingratiating" himself to whites is dismissed by Malcomson as a "shrewd" assessment of himself. This thought process is reminiscent of the way Michael Jordan (or any number of Blacks who gain wide acceptance among white audiences) has often been deemed different, unique, transcending Blackness, not like the rest of them, or as Malcomson not so eloquently put it, along with his foot in his mouth, "We have never had a politician quite like this. It may be a paradox, but only someone this rare could be so universal." Sound familiar?

Against all odds we must organize across race. Hip-hop is the last hope for this generation and arguably the last hope for America. The political elite has done an exceptional job of polarizing the country—liberal versus conservatives, Blacks versus whites, underclass versus elite, heterosexual versus homosexual. On every issue, mainstream electoral politics follows a strategy of divide and conquer. This is what allows our electoral system to function unchallenged as a private piggy bank for the rich. With most Americans locked out and opting out, American democracy has become democracy for the few. Nearly half of potential voters have given up on the electoral system, a point driven home by Ferai Chideya's *Trust: Reaching the 100 Million Missing Voters and Other Selected Essays* (2004).* The 60 percent voter turnout we witnessed in 2004 was the highest since 1968. The remaining disaffected voters could be pulled in, not only for races deemed crucial but for the long run, if we in the hip-hop voting bloc can demonstrate a politics that works for the many. To that end, a successful hip-hop political movement has something in it, not only for the hip-hop voting bloc but for the country at large—the vast majority of Americans who are locked out of the process, whether opting out altogether or voting for the lesser of the evils. So as labor unions and seniors bear witness to a hip-hop political movement unleashing new ways of organizing across race, they too will be empowered to explore similar strategies. The best remedy for leaving the old racial politics on the pages of history is a successful hip-hop political movement. Now more than ever, we don't have to buy into the old racial politics. We no longer have to settle for democracy for the few. This generation, as its cultural movement turns to politics, is creating for us all another choice.

---

*"In midterm elections, three-quarters of eligible voters routinely stay home."

Acknowledgments

Special thanks to Haki R. Madhubuti for the title and for always pushing me to go beyond the expected. Meggan Burnett for suggesting the concept. Cheryl Matthews for transcribing interviews. Ashley White-Stern and Katrina Phillips for research assistance. Sarah McNally Jackson, my original editor on this project. Marie Brown, my agent, for being much, much more than an agent. Chester Grundy for his mentorship, friendship and example and for turning me on to Bill Yousman's piece "Blackophilia and Blackophobia: White Youth, the Consumption of Rap Music and White Supremacy." My lifelong mentors, Larry Crowe, Dr. Fred Hord, Dr. Julius Thompson, Dr. Anderson Thompson, Dr. Ted Williams, Dr. Yvonne Williams, Dr. Carol Lee and Hannibal Afrik. Brother Mike Dyson for raising the bar on hip-hop journalism. Marc Anthony Neale, Murray Foreman, Marcyliena Morgan, Carlito Rodriquez, Billy Wimsatt, Mattie Weiss, Yvonne Bynoe, M-1, Riggs Morales, Wendy Day, Laura Ciocia, Joan Morgan, Akiba Solomon, Todd Boyd,

Michael Coburn, Heather Dickenson, Zoe Chace, Thabiti Lewis, Forrest Robinson, Nicole Balin, Will Patterson, Jeremy Miller, Taylor Vecsey, T. Denean Sharpley-Whiting, Mary Pattillo, Boots Riley, Chuck D, Lisa Ann Nevins, Kyle Stewart, Denise Paultre, Jeffrey Montgomery, Rob Biko Baker, Brother Kofi, Giuseppe Pipitone, Kim Jack Riley, Lee Copeland and the many, many other hip-hop coconspirators I've dialogued with over the years.

Also, to college students across the country who shared valuable insight into what brought them to hip-hop.

And to the example of the organizing committee of the first-ever National Hip-Hop Political Convention: Angela Woodson, Ras Baraka, T. J. Crawford, Baye Adofo Wilson, Rosa Clemente, Scott Heath, Geoff Ward, Alondo Reeves, Will Patterson, Antoine Seals, Alexis McGill, Damien Jackson, Hashim Shomari, Dawn-Elissa Fischer, James Bernard, Dereca Blackmon, Jeff Chang, Jeff Johnson, Billy Wimsatt, Thabiti Boone, David Kelly, Rev. Sekou, Van Jones, Davey D Cook and the countless local organizers across the country who contributed their time, resources and energy to making the convention possible.

Index